The Paraeducator in the Elementary School Classroom

Diane R. Page

Illustrations by Bruce Bigelow

The Scarecrow Press, Inc.
A Scarecrow Education Book
Lanham, Maryland, and London
2001

SCARECROW PRESS, INC.
A Scarecrow Education Book

Published in the United States of America
by Scarecrow Press, Inc.
4720 Boston Way, Lanham, Maryland 20706
www.scarecroweducation.com

4 Pleydell Gardens, Folkestone
Kent CT20 2DN, England

Copyright © 2001 by Diane R. Page

All rights reserved. No part of this publication may be reproduced, stored in a retrieval system, or transmitted in any form or by any means, electronic, mechanical, recording, or otherwise, without the prior permission of the publisher.

ISBN: 0-8108-3871-0

♾™ The paper used in this publication meets the minimum requirements of American National Standard for Information Sciences—Permanence of Paper for Printed Library Materials, ANSI/NISO Z39.48–1992.
Manufactured in the United States of America.

introducing

E. Cat

the

paraEduCator

All illustrations are reproduced with permission from
Sundown Studio, Inc., Bruce Bigelow, president and illustrator, April 2000.

I dedicate this book to

Sharon Davis
and
Carolyn Smith

two outstanding elementary classroom
assistant teachers.

We were

one thought,

one heartbeat,

one voice.

Acknowledgments

I would like to express my appreciation to the many teachers and their assistants who encouraged me to produce this manuscript. I am grateful for the special attention given to this effort by Dr. Joan Harlan, Vafa Jamasbi, Jean Vickers, Michelle Harris, Deborah Page, and my wonderful daughter, Elizabeth Tyer.

A special thank you goes to a very talented young man, John Clark Poole. His sketches of a most amusing adult cat to depict the elementary classroom assistant teacher directed graphic design artist Bruce Bigelow's creation of E. Cat. This feisty feline injects a flow of humor into what would have otherwise been a much too serious book.

Lastly, I express my heartfelt gratitude to Bruce. His patience, understanding, and enormous artistic abilities have made the production of *The Paraeducator in the Elementary School Classroom* a truly unique pleasure.

Contents

Introduction

Far too often elementary classroom assistant teachers are the "Forgotten Force" in Education. I seriously doubt if any of you experienced assistants were provided training by local school districts. You were expected to automatically know your job responsibilities and immediately perform those responsibilities quite well. Common sense dictates this just does not happen. How many other professions employ unskilled or semi-skilled labor and provide no training? You have a very special place and you have a very important position. Guidelines and performance expectations must be made available to you.

This book is for inexperienced elementary classroom assistant teachers. However, experienced assistant teachers will find helpful information and a validation of the importance of the responsibilities that are theirs every day.

A commonly heard statement made by many elementary classroom teachers is, "There's nothing better than a good assistant." That declaration is resoundingly true. Your professional growth, to provide a quality education for all children, was my commitment in writing this book.

Your position has several titles:

Teacher Aid(e)s
Assistant Teachers
Teacher Assistants
Paraeducators
Paraprofessionals

They all mean the same.

You!

Are you beginning to feel important?

You should.

You are!

My best wishes as you move beyond good
and become outstanding.

Diane Page

About the Book

The Paraeducator has three sections. Section One defines who you are as an elementary classroom assistant teacher. Section Two explains what is happening in American elementary school classrooms. Definitions and explanations are given for trends and issues that may not be familiar to you. Section Three is written especially for you and your teacher. Yes, The Paraeducator does end with this section, but exploring the many possibilities that exist for the two of you working together as a team only begins. At the back of this book you will find the Paraeducator Notebook. These pages are reproducible for your convenience.

The Paraeducator is an unfinished work. By no means do I have all the answers. Many times I have questions that can only be answered by you and your classroom teacher. I have provided wide margins for your questions, notes, and comments. At the end of most chapters are suggestions for you to complete the work I have started. I will give you general information and you will provide the specific. We will coauthor. No one will read over your shoulder. No one will grade you. Relax and have fun. You well deserve this time and space.

SECTION ONE

CHAPTER 1

Who Are You?

Welcome to the exciting world of children and learning. To outsiders your job as an elementary classroom assistant teacher looks easy.

"Just think, you go to work and leave work at reasonable hours."

"You have holidays and two or three summer months vacation time."

"The pay is poor but you have no responsibility of planning for the classroom."

These are comments you hear, and possibly, you have made. An assistant teacher's job is relatively easy.

Is it?

Surviving one full day of regular classroom activity changes your mind forever. By the end of the day you have a headache or a backache. Your feet are swollen and your bladder is popping. Dress shoes, no doubt, are in some corner. Your tie is torn or the makeup on your face has been wiped below your waist. Clean clothes donned in the morning are covered with paint, newsprint smudge, light to dark streaks of brown mud and various other spots and blobs of questionable, or of **no** definition.

Are you asking yourself, "Can it be **that bad**?"

It's not!

It's that good!

Because **you** were in the classroom today:

- **One child smiled.**

- **One child shared for the first time.**

- **One child made the lifelong connection between the spoken and the written word.**

**You
made positive differences
in the lives of children!**

———

Who are you?

———

**You
are
the main support system
for
the elementary classroom teacher!**

This statement is very important. Remember it. What you do, or what you do not do, directly affects the whole classroom environment.

Does this mean you are subordinate? No, this means you have a **supportive** position. Does this mean you are not due the respect from students the teacher gets? No, you have a right to earn just as much respect and to be promoted in this endeavor by your teacher. Does this mean you are not due the respect from parents the teacher gets? No, you have a right to earn their respect, too. Does this mean you must always agree with your teacher? No, this means you and your teacher must have communication skills in place to help you work through disagreements.

To better understand the role you play today in elementary school classrooms, a look into the past is helpful. Understanding your history gives needed insight into expectations of your role today.

American public school administrators first enlisted assistant teachers in the 1950s. There was a shortage of teachers and class sizes were large. Additional personnel were needed to help teachers with clerical duties and routine housekeeping chores. Teachers needed to spend more instructional time with students; however, minimum funds for hiring new personnel added to this dilemma. Consequently, aids were employed, working for very low wages, to perform non-instructional tasks in elementary school classrooms.

In 1964 the Great Society era began. President Lyndon B. Johnson's administration placed strong emphasis on domestic issues. Congress passed Johnson's proposal for increased federal money to education and never before in America's history had so much money been allocated for state and local use.

As a result, new demands were placed on our public elementary schools. Programs for disadvantaged pupils, services for handicapped students, more educational opportunities for racial minorities, and the delivery of these new programs and services added a different dimension to the roles of the teachers and the teacher aids. In addition to clerical and housekeeping duties, classroom teachers desperately needed their aids to help with instruction, too. Hence, the "Assistant Teacher" title was adopted.

In the late 1970s and in the early 1980s, the function of the assistant for instructional purposes became essential. Educators agreed this new role required adequate training and appropriate feedback. Once again, very little funding was made available for elementary classroom assistant teacher training or, for that matter, any assistant teacher professional development. Training, if provided by local districts, was often a one-day staff development program, leaving teachers and their assistants frustrated and confused. For the most part, assistant teacher training was left to elementary classroom teachers who considered this yet another burden placed on them.

In their book, *Using Paraeducators Effectively in the Classroom*, the authors (Pickett, Vasa, and Steckelberg) suggest that because of your expanded responsibilities and the importance of your presence in the elementary school classroom, the title "Paraeducators" more adequately describes what you have become over the last forty years. They equate the importance of this position to your counterparts in law and in medicine who are designated as "Paralegals" and "Paramedics."

I wholeheartedly agree!

Educating young children today is more challenging than ever before. In years past, teachers gave out knowledge in neat packages labeled "subjects" or "classes." Now they prepare and empower students to be "knowledge inventors." Added to this total restructuring of how and what students know and learn, elementary school educators have no choice but to accept the awesome responsibility of working with children every day who are heavily burdened with "societal" problems - drugs, violence, alcohol, sexual abuse, gangs, etc.

You and your teacher are mandated to be miracle workers. Your charge is to take all children who enter your classroom, many with special needs, and make effective, productive, educated citizens of them. For you to accept this challenge, you **must** know your job expectations.

- Remember -

You
    are
        the main support system
            for your
                elementary classroom teacher!

Simply stated, since the 1950s nothing has been deleted from your job list. More and more responsibilities have been added. Sadly, one thing has remained the same. You still work for extremely low wages. Nationwide, every year highly qualified elementary classroom assistant teachers seek employment elsewhere because of the monthly paycheck. Hopefully your district realizes your worth and pays accordingly.

Can you and your teacher truly be miracle workers?

Yes!

Miracles **do** happen every day in classrooms throughout America when teachers are assured their assistants are

capable

and

competent!

YOUR TURN

RESEARCH AND WRITE THE HISTORY OF THE
ELEMENTARY SCHOOL ASSISTANT TEACHER
IN THE SCHOOL DISTRICT WHERE YOU ARE
EMPLOYED.

_____

_____

_____

_____

_____

_____

_____

_____

_____

_____

_____

_____

_____

_____

_____

CHAPTER 2

Are You Qualified?

There are two types of "being qualified" for the position of elementary classroom assistant teacher - **external qualifications** and **internal qualifications**.

Let's investigate further.

Most states, therefore most school districts, require a high school diploma or a GED certificate for employment. Also, you may have been asked to submit a short essay for your employment file, along with a job application form and a medical form completed by your physician. You probably were asked for a list of personal and professional references. Some districts require a formal interview with either the director of personnel or with an elementary school principal. Obviously, whatever you did worked.

Congratulations!

You are now an elementary classroom assistant teacher!

Some of you had training after high school or after obtaining your GED. Many community colleges offer an associate arts degree in child development technology or education courses designed specifically for the elementary classroom assistant teacher position. Others of you have bachelor degrees from four-year colleges or universities in elementary education or in early childhood education. But, because of the law of supply and demand, you were unable to get a contract teaching position in a school district. You decided to "go the assistant teacher route" hoping that one day soon a contract position will open for you. A few of you are experienced classroom teachers, who for whatever reasons, have decided to "assist" in the classroom. There is a growing trend for retired teachers to accept the paraeducator role. Also, some parents, especially mothers who are trained to work in other professions, accept paraeducator positions during the time their children are in school.

Whatever your **external** qualifications happen to be,

- Remember -

You are now the main support system for your elementary classroom teacher!

WAIT!

STOP!

Oh, no.
This is not a contest!

This is not a "My degree is higher than your degree." - or - "My years of experience are more than yours!"

First,
you must pass
THE ACID TEST.

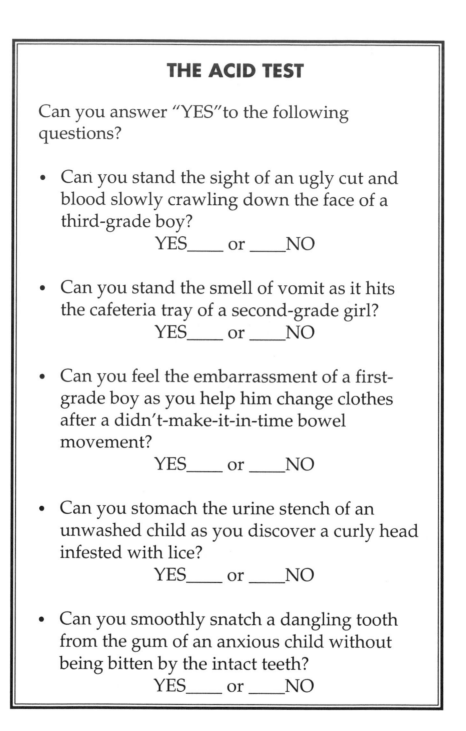

THE ACID TEST

Can you answer "YES" to the following questions?

- Can you stand the sight of an ugly cut and blood slowly crawling down the face of a third-grade boy?

  YES____ or ____NO

- Can you stand the smell of vomit as it hits the cafeteria tray of a second-grade girl?

  YES____ or ____NO

- Can you feel the embarrassment of a first-grade boy as you help him change clothes after a didn't-make-it-in-time bowel movement?

  YES____ or ____NO

- Can you stomach the urine stench of an unwashed child as you discover a curly head infested with lice?

  YES____ or ____NO

- Can you smoothly snatch a dangling tooth from the gum of an anxious child without being bitten by the intact teeth?

  YES____ or ____NO

That, my friends, is

THE ACID TEST.

These events do not happen every day. Nonetheless, they do happen. They strike fear in the hearts of children. You must be a source of safety and comfort for the child while acting in a **responsible, adult manner.**

No matter how many degrees you may have, no matter how much experience you may have, **if you cannot tolerate the event, and if you cannot help the child maintain his/her dignity through the event, then you need to quickly look elsewhere for employment.**

Thank you!

Now, you may continue reading.

Let's explore **internal** qualifications. Look at yourself. Be reflective. Remember, none of us is perfect. You will notice strong areas and weak areas. Keep the strong ones strong and do something now about correcting the weak ones.

The Twelve Mighty Musts
for
Paraeducators

Assistant teachers **must** enjoy working with others - children and adults. You do not have to be Mr. or Ms. Personality every day, but you do have to be a people person.

Assistant teachers **must** be reliable and dependable. Be at school on time in the mornings and leave school at the appointed time in the afternoons. Do use your common sense. If your teacher asks you to stay an extra five or ten minutes to finish a project, put a smile on your face and do it. Plan on conducting personal business during off-school hours. Errands should be run either before or after school. The same is true for using the telephone. Naturally, there will be times when making a telephone call is necessary, but keep these calls to a minimum. Also, ask family members and friends to limit their calls to calls of extreme importance, and certainly, emergency calls. You are paid by the school district to do school business.

Assistant teachers **must** adhere to school district sick and personal leave policies. Should you come to school with a high fever?

Absolutely not!

Notify your teacher or your principal as soon as you have made the decision to stay home. Each district allocates a specific number of sick leave days per year for contracted and for salaried personnel. Some districts allow teachers and assistants leave time to care for family members who are ill. Know the policy in place for your school district.

What about personal leave? Your district has a personal leave policy, too. Most school administrators ask, if possible, for you to get advance permission for a personal leave day. Yes, emergencies do arise and most principals and teachers are sensitive and caring.

- Just remember -

Use but do not abuse sick and/or personal leave.

Assistant teachers **must** comply with the district's dress and conduct codes. Be well-groomed. Does this mean you have to wear expensive clothes and shoes? No, this does mean you care enough about yourself to look the best you can. Does this mean you have to look like a teacher (whatever that is)? No, your personal style should never be taken away, but you do have a responsibility to dress professionally. Men, wear those ties - the brighter the better - not every day, but two or three times a week.

Many times what you wear to the elementary school classroom is directed by activities that will occur during the school day - activity-appropriate clothing. Also, many teachers and their assistants dress in costumes or wear clothing with holiday motifs to enhance the instructional program.

Children like colors, patterns, and bold designs. Children are going to touch you. They learn by feeling. They need to feel the textures of your clothes, your skin, and your hair. They want to remember the good way you smell. Use aftershave or cologne lightly.

Look nice!

Smell nice!

Brush your teeth!

If you should forget, you will quickly be reminded. Children are your best and your worst critics. They are direct and honest.

"Gosh, your breath stinks!"

"Your clothes look funny!"

"You smell bad!"

"You wore those same clothes yesterday!"

Remarks like these hit you
right between the eyes.

——

Personal habits - smoking, dipping or chewing tobacco, drinking alcohol or beer, using unlawful drugs - have no place in an elementary school, on an elementary school campus, on school busses, or at any school-related or school-sponsored function.

——

Assistant teachers **must** be flexible and adaptable. When unexpected events occur in an elementary school classroom, labored-over lesson plans are changed, reversed, abbreviated, or deleted. Children sense your aggravation and tension. They catch on quickly if you are stressed without your having to tell them and they react accordingly. Know your school's evacuation procedures for fires, tornadoes, hurricanes, earthquakes, bomb threats, and other disasters. In an actual emergency it is absolutely **essential** that you calmly flex and adapt. **Lives may depend on your ability!**

 Assistant teachers **must** exhibit self-control. Expressions of anger and hostility are not tolerated in the elementary classroom. At some time during the school year, you will be angry with one or more students and you will be angry with your teacher. You are only human. However, how you handle that anger is paramount. It is perfectly acceptable to say, "I am very angry (upset) right now! I need five or ten minutes cool-down time," or "What you did made me very angry! Let's talk about your behavior when I calm down." If you channel those feelings in "I" terms, then you model open, honest, and acceptable behaviors for the students and for other adults.

The count-to-ten rule works, too.

 Assistant teachers **must** be willing to accept constructive criticism. Listen carefully to your teacher. He/she may give you liberty to "do things your way." However, there are some jobs that must be done a certain way and there are some teachers who want you to do things "their way," especially when you first begin working together. **Cooperate!** Show your teacher that you are creative, resourceful, thoughtful, and enthusiastic. In no time at all your teacher will give you more and more control of the "what to do's" and the "how to do's."

 Assistant teachers **must** be willing to grow professionally. Yes, this does take extra time, with little, if any additional pay. Attend staff development programs, workshops, out-of-district visits, or other learning experiences planned for you.

———

The last four Musts are personal and may be very sensitive concerns. If you are lacking in any of these four areas, please do not hesitate to get help. Tell your teacher, building principal, or a close friend you realize you have deficiencies, and make a commitment to change.

———

Assistant teachers **must** speak clearly, using standard English patterns. If English is a second language, then the primary language must be spoken in standard patterns during the transition to English.

 Assistant teachers **must** write legibly. You may need practice sessions in manuscript and in cursive letter formation.

 Assistant teachers **must** spell commonly used words correctly.

 Assistant teachers **must** work basic mathematic problems correctly. Calculators are acceptable in most schools now.

———

Are you qualified?

Do you have what it takes?

YOUR TURN

READ **THE TWELVE MIGHTY MUSTS** ONE
MORE TIME, PLEASE. PICK **ONE** OF THE
TWELVE YOU FEEL NEEDS IMPROVING. IN
THE SPACE PROVIDED, WRITE AN ACTION
PLAN FOR THAT IMPROVEMENT. YOU MAY
NEED HELP DEVELOPING THIS PLAN. IF YOU
DO, ASK YOUR TEACHER, THE PRINCIPAL, OR
A CLOSE ASSOCIATE FOR HELP. BE SURE TO
INCLUDE A TIME LINE FOR IMPROVEMENT.
AT THE END OF THREE TO FOUR WEEKS,
CHECK YOUR PROGRESS.

_____

_____

_____

_____

_____

_____

_____

_____

_____

_____

_____

_____

Commonly Used Words

     The possibility of listing all commonly used words is virtually impossible. "The Basic Sight Word Vocabulary," by Dr. Edward Dolch, dates back to 1942. Dr. Dolch is considered one of the "greats" in the history of the Education profession. Although this chart was constructed in 1942, it still has meaning today. **It has stood the test of time.** On first glance you think, "I can spell those words!" You probably can. But did you know many times these words are misspelled by adults?

DOLCH BASIC SIGHT WORD VOCABULARY

THE BASIC SIGHT WORD TEST ON THE BASIC SIGHT VOCABULARY, Dolch, E., 1969.
Reproduced with permission of The McGraw-Hill Companies, Two Penn Plaza, New York, New York 10121-2298.

by	at	a	it
in	I	be	big
did	good	do	go
all	are	any	an
had	have	him	drink
its	is	into	if
ask	may	as	am
many	cut	keep	know
does	goes	going	and
has	he	his	far
but	jump	just	buy
black	kind	blue	find
fast	first	ate	eat
help	hot	both	hold

brown	grow	bring	green
four	every	found	eight
from	make	for	made
around	funny	always	because
long	let	little	look
away	again	after	about
cold	can	could	clean
full	fall	five	fly
before	best	better	been
live	like	laugh	light
her	here	how	hurt
down	done	draw	don't
give	get	gave	got
came	carry	call	come
sit	me	to	the
not	of	we	so
red	too	seven	walk
six	start	show	stop
put	round	right	pull
no	on	or	old
yellow	you	your	yes
please	pick	play	pretty
take	ten	they	today
my	much	must	together
own	under	off	over
out	new	now	our
open	one	only	once
try	myself	never	two

us	up	upon	use
with	white	was	wash
shall	she	sleep	small
who	write	would	why
some	very	sing	soon
wish	well	work	will
ran	read	run	ride
then	tell	their	them
see	saw	say	said
that	there	these	three
when	which	where	what
thank	those	this	think
want	went	were	warm

- Suggestion -

Keep a running list of other words that are new to you and are hard to spell. This is a wonderful behavior to model for children.

CHAPTER 3

What Can You Expect?

Chapter 3 is divided into three parts. The first part identifies general responsibilities of the elementary classroom assistant teacher. The second part addresses secretarial duties and the third part is, yes, you guessed it, to be written by you. If possible, your teacher should be part of the **YOUR TURN** activity. Only the two of you know tasks that are specific to your situation.

Wait! Stop! Do not panic!

I know what you did.

You looked ahead at the number of jobs listed in the first and second parts and you said to yourself, **"This is not for me! This is only chapter 3 and I'm expected to do all this? You've got to be kidding!"**

You did not have an anxiety attack, just a normal reaction. You will not be asked to perform all of these tasks every day. Just go ahead and read. When you are asked, you will feel comfortable knowing this is part of your job.

GENERAL RESPONSIBILITIES

You will:

- supervise students on field trips.
- help with bus and playground duty.
- help students at the water fountain or in the bathrooms.
- supervise students in the cafeteria.
- help students with classroom housekeeping.
- supervise rest periods for younger students.
- weigh and measure students (usually twice a year).
- assist students in the media center or in the computer lab.
- help students publish and display their work.
- assist students with project work.
- help prepare and decorate for special programs or events - example - Open House, PTA.
- attend parent-teacher conferences.
- care for younger brothers and sisters during parent-teacher conferences.
- assist the teacher in caring for a sick or an injured student - go for the principal, or call a parent.

- ready materials and equipment for a lesson and store them after the lesson.
- set up learning centers, cooking activities, and science experiments.
- mix paints and wash brushes for the art center.
- make minor repairs - the hammer/nail, screw/screwdriver kind.
- help students care for inside pets.
- help put the room in order at the end of the day and ready the room for the next day.

Yes, there is so much to do and seemingly so little time. By now you are wondering how teachers would survive without their assistants. Do you feel you are important?
Well, you should.

You are!

SECRETARIAL DUTIES

You will:
- help with school registration.
- make name tags.
- type letters and reports.
- run the copying machine.
- type narratives for portfolio assessments.
- collect money for school pictures or classroom projects.

- Suggestion -

Do not leave money in the classroom. Be sure to keep all money in the school safe.

- collect cafeteria tickets/money and complete a cafeteria report. Some school cafeterias use student credit cards. Yes, you may spend additional time helping students look for lost cards or investigating if a card has been stolen.
- record and report absent students.
- file.
- record grades.
- make and/or help students make general or specific portfolios.
- organize and/or help students organize items and information in portfolios.
- check out books and other materials and equipment from the media center.
- score tests using a scoring key.
- make inventory lists of materials and supplies.
- order supplies for the classroom.
- maintain and file health/immunization records.
- take notes during a teacher-planning meeting.

- Suggestion -

Use a tape recorder.
After the meeting check to be sure you have
recorded correctly.

- collect and organize materials for thematic units.
- send notes home to parents.
- collect forms sent from home.

- Suggestion -

Sometimes children bring forms back to school
unsigned. Always check to see if correct
signatures are present.

- telephone parents or guardians of children who are absent - **teacher request only.**
- telephone parents or guardians to remind them of conferences or meetings - **teacher request only.**

If you have computer skills, you are blessed. If you do not, don't worry. Students will be more than happy to teach you.

You are a learner, too!

YOUR TURN

THE GENERAL RESPONSIBILITIES AND THE SECRETARIAL DUTIES LISTED ARE **NOT** INCLUSIVE. IF POSSIBLE, YOU AND YOUR TEACHER COMPLETE THIS CHAPTER. IF NOT, ASK AN EXPERIENCED ELEMENTARY CLASSROOM ASSISTANT TEACHER TO WORK WITH YOU. IF THIS IS YOUR FIRST YEAR, YOU WILL NEED GUIDANCE. LIST OTHER RESPONSIBILITIES AND DUTIES THAT ARE YOURS IN YOUR CLASSROOM.

_____

_____

_____

_____

_____

_____

_____

_____

_____

_____

_____

_____

_____

_____

CHAPTER 4

What about Instruction?

The teacher is the instructional leader in the classroom. He/she plans for instruction and directs children as they learn.

Your **number one** responsibility in the instructional process is to **increase the effectiveness of your teacher.**

What does this mean?

You **increase** teacher effectiveness when you **increase** the **instructional interaction time between the teacher and the students.**

How does this work?

Let's use an example that occurs frequently in the elementary school classroom. The teacher asks the students who are working on a science project to gather their materials and come to the round table. All of the students, except Andy, scurry to the table with their reports, posters, books, paper, and colors. The assistant notices Andy sitting on the floor by his cubby sniffling and fighting back tears. Instead of the teacher leaving the already assembled group of students, the assistant goes over to help Andy. Andy tells the assistant that in their hurry to get to school on time, his twin brother, Randy, had mistakenly picked up his Science folder. Andy and the assistant walk down the hall to Mrs. Chambers's room and the missing Science folder is retrieved. Andy takes his place with the other students and the teacher. Now all is well.

But you say, "This is such a little thing." Yes, you are correct. However, if a time record were kept for a month, or even for a week, you would be amazed how the total number of teacher minutes **saved** would accrue.

Teacher effectiveness is also enhanced when you help students:
- enjoy learning.
- get along with others while learning.
- learn concepts and generalizations.
- function in a group democratically.
- develop self-confidence.
- widen their interests.
- resolve conflicts with other students.
- recognize that you are an excited learner.

What is **good instruction?** Effective teachers, regardless of their teaching styles, use six basic instructional strategies to design each lesson. What are these strategies? They are:

- a clear, attainable lesson objective,
- a dynamic presentation of the lesson,
- planned, guided practice for students,
- successful, independent practice for students,
- a comprehensive lesson review,

- and -

- student evaluation and lesson evaluation.

Excellent lesson design is only the beginning. Effective teachers plan for **Maximum Student Learning (MSL)**, too. No matter how well written the lesson plan, they know **MSL** occurs only for students when:

- they are actively engaged in the learning task.
- they are positively reinforced.
- they receive prompts (hints), wait time to think of a response, and they have immediate response feedback.
- they share what they know with other students and with other adults.
- they are given the freedom to learn authentic information independently and cooperatively.

- they are challenged by higher-order questions.
- they are in a safe, secure learning environment.

Be a **teacher watcher!** Watch how your teacher pulls a lesson plan from the page of a lesson plan book and makes it come alive for the students.

You must also be what Ken and Yetta Goodman call a **"kid watcher."** Know and understand each student's needs, interests, and abilities.

———

All students can learn!

Not all students learn in the same way

or at the same rate of speed,

but

they **do** learn!

———

What GENERAL **INSTRUCTIONAL** RESPONSIBILITIES will you have?

You will:

- work with small groups in activities that have been initiated by the teacher.
- assist the teacher with large group, instructional activities.
- assist with makeup work when students have been absent from school.
- assist with work and activities for students needing extra help.
- read and/or tell stories to large groups, small groups, or individual students.
- listen to students read.
- write for students as they dictate their stories to you.
- assist with art activities.
- help with daily, weekly, and long-range instructional planning.
- prepare instructional materials - games, charts, posters, bulletins boards, folder activities, and learning center materials.
- participate in informing parents or guardians of a student's instructional progress.

- supply information in evaluating a student's portfolio.
- help students plan project work.
- help students collect materials for project work.
- help students organize materials for project work.

- teach

songs,

games,

and

finger-plays.

Not only must you be an observer of the teacher and the students, but also you **must** be a **good listener.** Listen to your teacher's directions to the students. Know what he/she expects from the students.

Listen to the students.

**Learn how they understand,
and
how they misunderstand!**

YOUR TURN

ASK A STUDENT OR A SMALL GROUP OF STUDENTS TO EXPLAIN HOW THEY LEARNED A PARTICULAR SKILL OR CONCEPT. SOLVING PROBLEMS IN MATH IS ALWAYS GOOD FOR THIS ACTIVITY. ANOTHER SUGGESTION: ASK A STUDENT TO EXPLAIN HOW HE/SHE CONSTRUCTED AN ART PROJECT. PROBE FOR UNDERSTANDING AND FOR MISUNDER-STANDING. TAPE RECORD THE CONVERSA-TION. WRITE DOWN WHAT THE STUDENT(S) TELLS YOU. YOU WILL BE SURPRISED!

_____

_____

_____

_____

_____

_____

_____

_____

_____

PART II

LIST INSTRUCTIONAL ACTIVITIES YOU ARE
COMFORTABLE WITH NOW. LIST
INSTRUCTIONAL ACTIVITIES YOU ARE NOT
COMFORTABLE WITH NOW. MAKE AN
ACTION PLAN WITH YOUR TEACHER TO
BECOME MORE SKILLED AND MORE
EFFECTIVE IN THE UNCOMFORTABLE
INSTRUCTIONAL AREAS.

COMFORTABLE ACTIVITIES:

_____

_____

_____

_____

_____

_____

_____

_____

_____

_____

_____

_____

UNCOMFORTABLE ACTIVITIES:

_____

_____

_____

_____

_____

_____

_____

ACTION PLAN:

_____

_____

_____

_____

_____

_____

_____

_____

_____

_____

CHAPTER 5

What Are Professional Relationships? Why Are They Important?

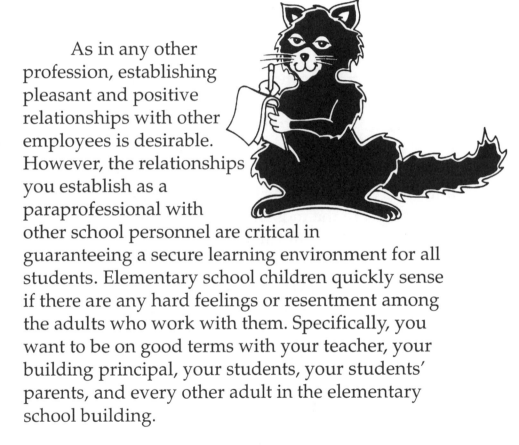

As in any other profession, establishing pleasant and positive relationships with other employees is desirable. However, the relationships you establish as a paraprofessional with other school personnel are critical in guaranteeing a secure learning environment for all students. Elementary school children quickly sense if there are any hard feelings or resentment among the adults who work with them. Specifically, you want to be on good terms with your teacher, your building principal, your students, your students' parents, and every other adult in the elementary school building.

Let's take a closer look.

The Teacher

There must be evidence of **common**

- **understanding**
- **trust**
- **consideration**
- and **cooperation**

between you and your teacher. Time, or the lack of time, to communicate could cause conflict right from the start if you are not aware of the many pressing responsibilities your teacher has each and every day. Rarely does your teacher have enough time to address all the needs of his/her students and rarely does he/she have enough time to communicate the most important classroom assistant teacher information to you.

Often, inexperienced elementary classroom assistant teachers get their feelings hurt when it seems the teacher is ignoring them. Be assured - that teacher is **not** ignoring you. He/she is concentrating on the one million things that have to be done that school day.

Try to be understanding!

Buy a small, lined notebook. Write down your questions, concerns, and ideas. When you and your teacher have a planning time, or by chance, a few extra minutes, then discuss what you have written. Many teachers will already have a time planned for the two of you to conference.

Conflicts occur because of a breakdown in communication. If a conflict should arise, do not, I repeat, **do not** take the conflict outside of your classroom.

CONFLICT

ASSISTANT
TEACHER

TEACHER

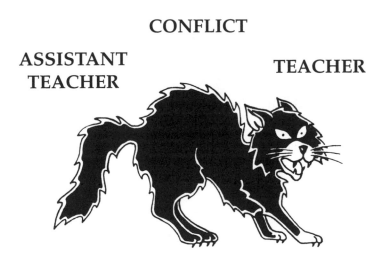

As human beings we are all tempted to run to others and declare how horrible old Mr./Ms. So-and-So is, what he/she did, and how you would have handled the situation. Teachers are not perfect and neither are you. Allow for everyone having a "bad day" now and then.

If a conflict should arise that warrants focused attention, arrange for a private time - away from the students - to discuss the situation with your teacher. Get the problem out in the open. Discuss the problem and work together on ways to correct the problem.

———

If, and only if, the conflict cannot be resolved by you and your teacher, ask the principal to intervene.

———

A quite descriptive and extremely realistic job description for an elementary teacher was published in the *Teachers Network News*, 1990, by the Harvard Graduate School of Education:

WANTED: ELEMENTARY TEACHER
Be Everything at Once

JOB OPENING

Looking for a:
  SELF-starting,
  SELF-propelled,
  SELF-confident,
  SELF-supporting,
  SELF-sufficient,
  SELF-promoting,
  SELF-cleaning,
  SELF-less individual.

MINIMUM wage guaranteed. Hours: 7:30 A.M.-4:00 P.M., plus evenings and weekends.

Average 60 stimulating hours per week-no over-time pay. Summers off(unless you have a mortgage or need a degree.)

Must be able to work independently in a chaotic, cooperative/competitive environment.

Applicant must have skills and knowledge in the following areas:

Diplomacy	Interior decorating	Psychology
Crowd control	Clerical procedures	Geography
Social work	Cooking	Computer literacy
Risk taking	Plumbing	Writing
Family therapy	Administration	History
Systems management	Aerobics	Math(new and old)
Communications	Legal affairs	Foreign languages
Time management	Acrobatics	Science
Motivational techniques	Acting	Literature
A V operation and repair	Pest control	Art appreciation
First aid	Accounting	Health
Bulletin board design	Carpentry	Music
Community building	Current affairs	Behavioral management

Some light housekeeping required. Sense of humor, compassion, and caring mandatory. Diplomatic, paramedic, and military experience helpful. Prior seminars in stress reduction useful. Flexibility and courage a must.

This does cause one to chuckle. Stop and think about all you see your teacher doing every day. Should you have to ask if your teacher needs more time? Should you have to ask if your teacher needs an assistant?

The Principal

The principal is the leader of the elementary school. Therefore, the principal is responsible for all that happens or does not happen in the school. Just as you and your teacher have a direct responsibility to your students, your building principal has a direct responsibility to all students, teachers, support staff, assistant teachers, parents, custodial staff, secretarial staff, cafeteria staff, and sometimes, those in charge of transportation - a busy person, indeed. Also, the principal works with other building principals and school administrators to ensure a cohesive instructional program district-wide. How can you develop a relationship with someone whose day is so heavily scheduled?

The best way possible is to work effectively with your teacher. Teachers brag most about their students, but secondly, they brag about their great assistants. The principal will definitely hear about you. How can you make the principal's job easier?

Always say positive statements about your school, in the school setting and out in the community! Also, know and follow school district policy!

The Students

You must work toward building good rapport with all students. Yes, some children are more likable than others. That only means you will have to work harder in really getting to know those children who send out the "Leave me alone!" message. As you work directly with each student, feelings of mutual confidence and respect will develop. **You cannot demand respect. You have to earn it.** Deal fairly and honestly with all students. Encourage and motivate each student based on each student's needs. You must be a good listener. Many students simply need an adult who will listen to them without passing judgment.

The Parents

To establish a successful relationship with the parents of students in your classroom, your primary job is to define for them your supportive role in the classroom. What does this mean? Many times parents are not sure what you actually do in the classroom. They merely see two adults working with their child. Explain what you do and how you do it. Naturally, answer their general questions, but if you are asked specific questions regarding the progress of the child or about a specific problem the child may be having, **always** refer them to the classroom teacher.

You are expected to make these referrals.
Your teacher will thank you!

Confidentiality

As an elementary classroom assistant teacher, you may be privileged to information about students that you absolutely, positively, must keep to yourself. In establishing the **best** learning environment for every student, your teacher will share information with you about students to better meet their individual needs. This should never be in the form of "talking about" the child but should be only information that serves to better the instructional program for the child.

**You cannot discuss this information
at school, at home,
or out in the community.
Your job security depends on this!**

Most building principals will quickly dismiss you if this trust is broken.

Am I trying to instill a grain of fear here?

Yes!

You are perfectly correct!

Other Adults

During the fast-paced school day you will not have much extra time to spend getting to know other adults in the building. Always smile, say "Hello," and practice the Golden Rule.

You may be asked to serve on a building committee, make a contribution for flowers, help prepare food to take to a teacher who has been in the hospital, or work at the school carnival. Is this part of your job? **Yes!**

Gladly participate in the activities of your elementary school. Yes, it is your school and you are a very important person in that school!

YOUR TURN

EVERYONE, YES, EVERYONE CAN DO AT
LEAST ONE THING VERY WELL. YOURS MAY
BE COOKING, BUILDING, PAINTING,
GARDENING, SEWING, CLEANING, WORKING
WITH THE COMPUTER, ETC. THINK OF THE
ONE THING THAT YOU CAN DO BEST. WRITE
IT DOWN IN THE SPACE PROVIDED. GO INTO
DETAIL IF YOU WISH. TALK TO YOUR
TEACHER ABOUT HOW YOU COULD
EFFECTIVELY USE THIS TALENT IN THE
CLASSROOM. WRITE DOWN YOUR TEACHER'S
SUGGESTIONS. THEN, **GET BUSY.**

THANK YOU!

_____

_____

_____

_____

_____

_____

_____

_____

_____

_____

CHAPTER 6

Are You Confused about Safety?

The safety of each child is the most important consideration in **any** activity.

Accidents do happen at school, but accidents should **never** occur because of neglect.

- **Never** leave students unattended, either in the classroom or on school grounds.
- **Never** assume the students will be safe by themselves.
- **Never** assume someone else is watching the students.

- Remember -

Needless conversation with other adults directs your attention away from the students in your charge.

Most accidents are preventable and school administrators, building principals, and teachers work extra hard establishing and maintaining safe classrooms, buildings, buses, playgrounds, and playground equipment.

A safe school building and school campus must be top priority!

If an accident should occur in your presence, **do not leave the child(ren).** If your teacher is not with you, send for him/her **immediately.** Keep with you at all times, in a purse or in a pocket, a small notebook with telephone numbers of students' parents/guardians. List work numbers, home numbers, and emergency call numbers. **Be sure these numbers are up-to-date.** Duplicate a book for your teacher, too. Also, take first aid and/or CPR courses when they are offered.

You will have hall, bathroom, cafeteria, and bus duty. Duty is just that. You are still on the job. Off duty is when you have break time.

Bus duty is often confusing, but it need not be. At the beginning of the school year, most teachers teach their students, especially the younger ones, how to find the correct bus and how to load and unload the bus safely. Students **do** forget and they should **not** be reprimanded for forgetting.

Patiently guide them!

If students are privately transported to and from school, it is **imperative** you know students are leaving school with the designated person(s). **Never assume anything here.** If you are ever unsure, take the student to the principal's office to wait. Discuss the problem with the principal, the vice principal, or a teacher. **You do not have the authority to let the student leave the school building.**

You hear about strangers abducting children, and yes, that does happen! However, most abductors are adults who know the children. In a divorce situation usually the court awards custody to one parent. Often a court order forbids the other parent from having any contact, or limited contact, with the child. Be sure your teacher has the correct information in writing from one or both parents. This information is usually kept in the school office and teachers have access to this information.

Am I suggesting that you be extremely careful?

Yes!

You are absolutely correct!

Many schools require visitors to the building to get a visitor's pass before entering the areas where the students are located. If this is your school's policy and if you see someone without a pass, it is your responsibility to stop and remind that person of the rule. Also, if you are asked to wear an employee identification badge, please do so willingly.

Both policies are good.

Support them!

Your Safety

The following situation should occur very rarely in your school; however, when an illness epidemic hits, all substitute teachers are quickly employed. The principal may ask you to take charge of your classroom or another teacher's classroom for the day. You may feel uneasy or hesitant about assuming this responsibility - but cooperate 100 percent! Do ask the principal to inform a teacher close by of the situation. Ask the principal to get that teacher to check on you from time to time during the day or to be on call in case **you** need help.

Also, the principal may ask you to close the school day for your teacher if the teacher has to leave school early to attend a meeting. Again, ask the principal to network you with another classroom teacher. This too should occur infrequently.

Be sure you know your school's policy concerning giving medication of any kind to students. Very often students will bring medication with them to school along with a note from home asking that you or your teacher give it to the child during the school day. Most school districts only allow a school nurse to give any form of medicine, including aspirin. Follow school policy here.

Latex (surgical) gloves should be worn whenever you come in contact with bodily fluids. This is a safety precaution for you, as well as for the student. Also, aprons or smocks should be worn to protect your clothing from bodily fluids, especially when working with younger students.

Teaching students safety rules
and
modeling safety measures for them

cannot be overstated!

As the **main** support system

for your teacher,

he/she must be confident

that you

never assume anything

and

never neglect anyone!

YOUR TURN

THINK ABOUT YOUR SCHOOL AND YOUR
PARTICULAR SITUATION. LIST SAFETY RULES
AND PRECAUTIONS YOU MUST PRACTICE
AND ENFORCE EVERY DAY.

_____

_____

_____

_____

_____

_____

_____

_____

_____

_____

_____

_____

_____

_____

_____

_____

Classroom Management
and
Discipline

Look at the clock!

Look at the teacher!

Do you feel this way, too?

"Miss Carolyn wore her 'No Nonsense' panty hose today!"

CHAPTER 7

What Do You Need to Know about Classroom Management and Discipline?

Every teacher has a classroom management plan. You say, "Oh no they don't!" I say, "Oh yes they do!" The key question is, "Do all teachers have **effective** classroom management plans?"

You are right!

Some do not!

What are students doing in **well-managed** classrooms?
- Students are highly motivated and involved in their learning.
- Students are on task. They know what is expected of them.
- Students experience success frequently.
- Students encounter very little wasted time, confusion, and/or disruptions.

- Students work together in caring for the classroom. A sense of pride and ownership is evident.

Well-managed classrooms just do not happen. Teachers establish well-managed classrooms.

Research conducted by Dr. Carolyn Evertson and Dr. Edmund Emmer found that effective classroom managers are **proactive** rather than **reactive**. These teachers do not simply deal with problems after they occur. They prevent problems from arising. They use a comprehensive management system that includes three major components:
- **Planning**
- **Implementing**
- **Maintaining**

Effective managers plan the room arrangement, the rules, and the procedures needed for a smoothly run classroom. Most teachers have rules and procedures, but effective managers **teach** these rules and procedures to their students with as much fervor as they teach instructional skills.

At every grade level effective managers:
- spend the first weeks of school introducing, reviewing, and practicing rules and procedures.

- communicate student behavior expectations to parents or guardians in writing.
- are consistent in maintaining the management system throughout the school year.
- give students choices. Students help write the rules, the procedures, and the consequences if rules and procedures are not followed.

Students know from the first day of school that if they obey the rules and follow the procedures, they will be rewarded. If they choose to disobey the rules, and if they choose not to follow the procedures, they must be willing to accept the consequences.

Drs. Joan and Peter Carson state in *Any Teacher Can!*, that "Effective classroom rules are short, positively stated, and easy for students to remember. Good classroom rules specifically summarize appropriate behavior and thus help students remember what is expected of them. A behaviorally stated rule as 'We walk in the halls' specifies appropriate behavior. Such rules help teachers (and assistants) prevent the occurrence of common classroom behavior problems because children know what behavior is expected of them.

Having rules stated in behavioral terms also makes students less likely to accidentally break the rules or ignore rules trying to 'see how much they can get away with' before being reprimanded."

These two experts also suggest posting rules and procedures in the classrooms and in the hallways. Students are easily reminded of appropriate behaviors when rules and procedures are clearly visible.

Effective classroom management establishes the right conditions for teaching and learning. Effective teachers prevent problems before they arise. They differ from those who are less effective not in how well they handle disruptive students but in how they establish and maintain well-run classrooms.

What is your responsibility?

Ask your teacher to explain his/her management system to you. Support the management system.

**Breakdown in communication
and teacher/assistant teacher conflict occur more
often from a lack of understanding classroom
management and discipline plans than from
a lack of understanding instructional plans.**

- A Word of Caution -

There will be times when you will not agree
with your teacher. You do not have to agree, but
you must **never** disagree in front of the students.
Plan a private time away from the students to
discuss and resolve the conflict.

- The **Last** Resort -

**What if the conflict absolutely cannot be
resolved?**

**What if you leave school every day
totally frustrated
because
you have been asked to support
a
management or discipline plan
that is contrary to your every belief?**

**In a private conference time
ask your principal to
please place you with another teacher
whose philosophy of management
and
discipline
is basically the same
as
yours.**

Most elementary school principals leave
classroom management to the classroom teacher.
Usually discipline policy and procedure is set by the
school district. Discipline is generally
considered:
- **Reactive**
- **Punishment**
- **Punitive action**

"If you do this, then I'll do that!"

- but -

Think for a moment.

Could **discipline** also include:
- showing children **positive**
  alternatives rather than just being told **"No"**?

- teaching children how their actions affect others?
- reminding children you want to reward good behavior?
- establishing **fair, simple rules** and **enforcing them consistently**?

Yes!   **Yes!**   **Yes!**

You are absolutely correct!

Research shows repeatedly that children who are **taught acceptable behavior:**
- **learn to share and cooperate.**
- **are better able to handle anger.**
- **are more self-disciplined.**
- **feel successful and in control of themselves.**

———

As you work with children every day **please** remember some forms of punishment can be very **sly** and **sneaky.** What does this mean? We know children are punished when:
- Their behavior is controlled through **fear. "Do you want five licks with the paddle?"**

- Their feelings are not respected.
  "Why can't you be smart like your sister?"

- They behave **only** to avoid a penalty or to get a bribe.
  "Students, if you misbehave while I'm gone to the office, you will not have recess for a whole week!"

Research also shows that children who are **repeatedly** and **severely** punished:
- tend to be aggressive, hostile, and angry.
  "I hate you! I wish you were dead!" Meko screams at his teacher.

- fail to develop self-control.
  "Let's steal these tennis balls! Ain't nobody watching!" Janie hurriedly whispers to Lauren.

- hide their mistakes.
  "I got all of 'em right!" Jeff reports to his teacher, although he incorrectly answered twelve math problems.

- feel humiliated.
  "I ain't never gonna 'mount to nothing. I ain't even gonna try."

In the real world of school, punishment does occur. What does punishment look like?

- **time-out from activities**
- **in-school suspension**
- **out-of-school suspension**
- **expulsion**
- **corporal punishment (spanking)**

Many school districts throughout the United States have banned corporal punishment. Their decisions are based on research that clearly states, study after study, corporal punishment **does not** work. If spanking is used, the inappropriate behavior may be halted temporarily, but:

- appropriate behaviors are not taught.
- adult violence is modeled for students.
- spanking may be considered a form of child abuse.

"Wait just a minute," you say. "I spank my own children."

That's your business. **In your paraeducator position, you absolutely do not have the right to inflict pain on another person's child.** If you do, you are throwing the doors wide open for legal action - a lawsuit - against you. Also, you have the right to refuse serving as witness to a child being spanked by a principal or a teacher. If a lawsuit should be brought against the principal or the teacher, and if you have served as a witness, then you may go to court, too.

- Remember -

Student behaviors closely mirror adult (teacher/assistant teacher) behaviors. Adult actions, attitudes, and expectations greatly influence what students believe and how students behave.

A teacher once remarked, "I don't know why these kids won't be quiet! I have yelled 'Be quiet!' at them twenty times."

You get the picture.

Corporal Punishment

Read the caption.

"When I grow up, I'm going to prison where spanking is cruel and unusual punishment!"

Do you want to:

a. _____ laugh?

b. _____ cry?

Praise
and
Rewards

Often praise and rewards are used **incorrectly.** Yes, this does happen. Dr. Anita Woolfolk suggests:

SPECIFIC

GUIDELINES

FOR

USING PRAISE APPROPRIATELY

Be clear and systematic in giving praise.
Examples

1. Make sure praise is tied directly to appropriate behavior and doesn't happen randomly.
2. Make sure the student understands the specific action or accomplishment that is being praised. You could say, "You brought the materials I lent you back on time and in excellent condition. Well done!" instead of saying, "You were very responsible."

Recognize genuine accomplishments.
Examples

1. Reward the attainment of specified goals, not just participation, unless participation is the major goal of the activity.
2. Be especially careful not to reward uninvolved students just for being quiet and not disrupting class.
3. Tie praise to students' improving competence or to the value of their accomplishment. You might say, "You are working more carefully now. I noticed that you double-checked all your problems. That is a very important habit to develop. Your score reflects your careful work," instead of simply, "Good for you. You have the top grade in the group."

Set standards for praise based on the individual abilities and limitations of the student involved.
Examples

1. Praise progress or accomplishment in relation to the individual student's past efforts.
2. Focus the student's attention on his or her own progress, not on comparisons with others.

Attribute the student's success to effort and ability, so the student will gain confidence that success is possible again.
Examples

1. Avoid implying that the success may be based on luck, extra help, or easy material.
2. Ask students to describe the problems they encountered and how they solved them.

Make praise really reinforcing.
Examples

1. Avoid singling out students for praise in an obvious attempt to influence the rest of the class. This tactic often backfires, since students know what's really going on. In addition, if you say, "I like the way Ken is . . ." too many times, Ken will be embarrassed and may be seen as the teacher's pet.
2. Don't give undeserved praise to students simply to balance failures. (Brophy calls this "praise as a consolation prize.") It is seldom consoling and calls attention to the student's inability to earn genuine recognition.

———

Realistically, you will seldom have time during the busy school day to give a specifically detailed praise statement to every student. Are a few quick words of genuine praise better than no words? Yes. "What can I say?" you ask.

———

Here are several suggestions.

Quick Praise Statements
for
Super Students

Now you've figured it out.
You haven't missed a thing.
Keep up the good work.
Nothing can stop you now!
EXCELLENT!
That's the best ever.
FINE!
You've got your brain in gear today.
WONDERFUL!
That's better than ever.
Nice going.
I like that.
I'm very proud of you.
I think you've got it now.
You figured that out fast.
That's really nice!
You're right!
CLEVER!
That's great!
Way to go!
Now you have the hang of it!

You're on the right track now!
You are very good at that.
That's very much better.
I'm happy to see you working like that.
You're doing a good job.
That's the best you've ever done.
I knew you could do it.
Now you've figured it out.
Now you have it.
GREAT!
Keep working on it. You're getting better.
You make it look easy.
That's the right way to do it.
You're getting better every day.
You're really growing up!
Nice going!
SENSATIONAL!
That's the way to do it.
That's better.
That's RIGHT!
That's GOOD!
When I'm working with you I
feel like singing!
GOOD WORK!
I'm proud of the way you worked
today.
You're really working hard today.
You've just about got it.
CONGRATULATIONS!

Are **Rewards** Always **Rewards?**

No.

Drs. Joan and Peter Carson remind us that rewards **must** maintain or strengthen a behavior. If a reward is given to a child and the behavior is **not** maintained or is **not** strengthened, then the reward has ceased to be a reward.

"A reward must be positive, rewarding, and pleasurable. **Satiation** occurs when a reinforcer (reward) loses its effectiveness because of its repeated use. A child, like everyone else, may tire of a certain reward. **A reward for one child will not necessarily be a reward for another child.**" (*Any Teacher Can!*)

Many times rewards are **age dependent.** For example, elementary school-age children usually like to have the teacher or the assistant teacher put happy stickers on their papers. However, most middle school students would **cringe** and experience **total embarrassment** if their papers were returned with happy stickers. What are appropriate rewards for elementary school students?

Elementary school students like rewards that are tangible. Suggestions include:

- Bookmarkers and erasers
- Small toys from a grab bag
- Stickers and pencils
- Candy
- Certificates of Achievement

Even though children like to get these, tangible rewards can be costly. Also, many teachers object to tangibles because they believe students will work just to get a prize. Often parents object, too.

Many rewards are not tangible and students like them, also. Suggestions include:

- Extra outside play time
- Homework passes
- Sitting by the teacher or assistant teacher at lunch
- A round of applause or a hug
- Extra reading time
- A special video or DVD
- Teacher's or Assistant Teacher's Helper
- Student of the Day or Student of the Week
- Going to a lower grade to read to students
- A note to the principal complimenting the student
- A pat on the back and a handshake

What you will probably observe in your classroom are many intangible rewards. Occasionally tangibles will be used. It is very important that you and your teacher agree on the rewards system.

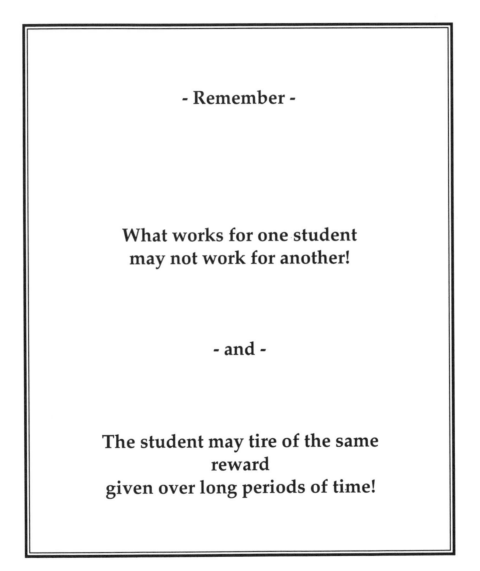

- Remember -

What works for one student may not work for another!

- and -

The student may tire of the same reward given over long periods of time!

YOUR TURN

WHAT IS YOUR SCHOOL'S/DISTRICT'S POLICY REGARDING CORPORAL PUNISHMENT (SPANKING)? WHAT IS YOUR TEACHER'S OPINION ABOUT CORPORAL PUNISHMENT? WHAT IS YOUR OPINION? WRITE YOUR ANSWERS ON THE FOLLOWING LINES.

_____

_____

_____

_____

_____

_____

_____

_____

_____

_____

_____

_____

_____

SECTION ONE

STUDY GUIDE

SECTION ONE
STUDY GUIDE

CHAPTER 1:

1. Explain the difference in the **supportive** position of the elementary classroom assistant teacher and a subordinate role position.

2. Discuss the history of the paraeducator movement in America.

3. Explain why educating children today is even more challenging than in years gone by.

4. Every year highly qualified assistant teachers leave the profession. Why?

5. Name the two **C's** that describe highly qualified elementary classroom assistant teachers.

CHAPTER 2:

1. Discuss the **external qualifications** of an elementary classroom assistant teacher.

2. Explain **THE ACID TEST.** Why is a "Yes" answer to each question so very important?

3. Discuss the **internal qualifications** of an

elementary classroom assistant teacher - **The Twelve Mighty Musts!**

CHAPTER 3:

1. List the **general responsibilities** of the elementary classroom assistant teacher.

2. List the **secretarial duties** of the elementary classroom assistant teacher.

CHAPTER 4:

1. Name the six basic instructional strategies teachers use for **good** instruction.

2. What is the **number one** responsibility of the elementary classroom assistant teacher in the instructional process?

3. Why is it important for students to recognize that the elementary classroom assistant teacher is an excited learner, too?

4. What are the **general instructional responsibilities** of the elementary classroom assistant teacher?

5. Why is it important for the assistant to **listen** carefully?

CHAPTER 5:

1. Elementary classroom assistant teachers and their classroom teachers must share a **common** bond in four areas. Name them.

2. If a conflict should arise between the assistant teacher and the teacher, what must be done?

3. List the three **best** ways the elementary classroom assistant teacher can be supportive of the principal.

4. Discuss the professional relationship between the assistant teacher and the students.

5. How should the assistant respond to a parent's question concerning his child's hostile behavior in the classroom?

6. What responsibility does the elementary classroom assistant teacher have regarding **confidentiality**?

CHAPTER 6:

1. Accidents should **never** occur because of neglect. Discuss this statement in detail.

2. If an accident should occur in the presence of the elementary classroom assistant teacher, what must be done?

3. Sally's grandfather transports her to and from school. One afternoon a nice gentleman who says he is Sally's uncle tells the assistant that her grandfather is at the dentist's office, and he is taking Sally home. What is the responsibility of the assistant?

4. Explain the necessity of supporting a visitor's pass policy and an employee identification badge policy.

5. Mrs. Leseur, the classroom teacher, received a telephone call from her husband telling her that their son had been involved in an automobile accident. She must leave school immediately. The principal asks the assistant to take charge of the classroom until the bell rings at the end of the day. What is the responsibility of the assistant?

6. Casius's sister wrote a note to the assistant teacher asking him to give Casius two aspirin if his head started hurting during the day. What is the responsibility of the assistant?

CHAPTER 7:

1. What are students doing in **well-managed classrooms?**

2. Explain **proactive** classroom management.

3. Explain **reactive** classroom management.

4. What are the three major components of a comprehensive classroom management system?

5. Why is being consistent and fair so necessary for effectiveness?

6. Explain what is meant by "behaviorally" stated rules (Carson and Carson).

7. Why should rules and procedures be posted in the classrooms and in the hallways?

8. What generally comes to mind when one hears the word discipline?

9. What else could discipline be?

10. Usually children who are taught acceptable behaviors exhibit certain characteristics. What are those characteristics?

11. Why should corporal punishment **never** be used as a form of punishment?

12. What characteristics do severely and repeatedly punished children exhibit?

13. Why should sarcasm **never** be used in the classroom?

14. Discuss Woolfolk's "Specific Guidelines for Using Praise Appropriately."

15. Many times rewards are age-dependent. Explain this statement.

16. Explain **satiation**.

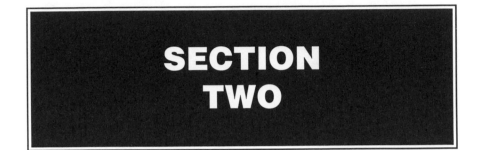

SECTION TWO

CHAPTER 8

What Does the Elementary School Look Like?

Do elementary schools resemble the elementary schools many of you attended? They may look much the same on the outside, but inside change is occurring. Are students' desks arranged in neat rows facing the teacher's desk located in front of the classroom? I think not. Desks have been replaced with tables and chairs. Students work in small groups - at tables, on the floor, outside the building, or in the hallway. They freely go from the classroom to the computer lab or media center.

Teachers and their assistants, once clearly visible, are now hard to spot. They are:

- sitting on beanbags readingto students.
- in the supply closet digging out cloth scraps for future puppets.

- helping students plant a vegetable garden.
- working with small groups of students on science experiments or on math projects.
- binding books written on school computers.

What happened to the familiar classroom?

Changes are rapidly taking place in all professions including Education. In today's high-tech, fast-paced world, could we say the only thing that is predictable and constant is change?

Teachers, principals, and school administrators often use words and terminology that baffle you. Not wanting to be embarrassed, you nod your head in either agreement or in disagreement, but you are still confused. Do you often leave a conversation wishing you knew more, but no one had the time, or took the time, to explain and elaborate?

Let's stop right now and clear away some cobwebs. After reading this chapter and chapter 9, you will better understand the technical jargon you hear every day.

A big buzzword today is **transition(s)**. Transition literally means the process of moving from one place, or position, to another. For the most part, school administrators nationwide want their classroom teachers to move from a traditional model toward a developmentally appropriate, child-centered model of teaching children. But, you ask, "What's wrong with the **old** way?"

Nothing!

No student ever died because they were - or are - in a traditional classroom.

Before we continue, we **must** address a **very common misunderstanding.**

Somehow, probably by what educators have recently said or implied, we seem to have the notion that teachers whose teaching styles are more traditional are not good teachers. This is not necessarily true. Also, we seem to believe that teachers whose teaching styles follow the developmentally appropriate, child-centered model are great teachers. This is not necessarily true either.

Be very careful here.

- Remember -
Don't judge a book by its cover.

There are **super** traditional teachers and there are **not-so-super** developmentally appropriate practices teachers. There are **super** developmentally appropriate practices teachers and there are **not-so-super** traditional teachers.

Let's continue.

In the past ten years, researchers investigating how children learn, strongly suggest children learn much better and much more when teachers believe in developmentally appropriate practices and implement the developmentally appropriate, child-centered model in their classrooms. Authors Bredekamp, Schwartz, and Pollishuke have written extensively on this subject.

Imagine, if you will, two extreme opposites. Very rarely will you see a pure traditional classroom and very rarely will you see a pure developmentally appropriate one. What you will observe are teachers using a mixture of traditional methods and developmentally appropriate practices. Each teacher's style is unique; however, most teachers are working toward, or making the transition, from the teacher-centered philosophy to the child-centered philosophy.

**The Teacher-Centered
(Traditional)
Philosophy
embraces the following ideas:**

- **Teaching is fact-oriented.**
- **Emphasis is placed on how many facts are known and how these facts are defined.**
- **Teaching is skills-based.**
- **Parts of information are given to students. Then, students are expected to transfer these parts to a whole (idea or concept).**
- **Learning is seen as a passive activity.**
- **Heavy emphasis is placed on mastery of facts.**
- **Students are tested often, and their test scores are compared to a set standard of achievement.**

The Child-Centered
(Developmentally Appropriate)
Philosophy
includes the following beliefs:

- Students move beyond facts and are encouraged to interact with the unknown.
- Students are taught strategies for constructing meaning.
- Emphasis is placed on actual thinking through a problem or situation. This is called process learning.
- Teachers believe children basically learn from whole to part. What does this mean? If ants and an ant farm are totally fascinating to a child, then learning the body parts of an ant will probably be something the child will want to know. On the other hand, making twenty children learn the parts of an ant's body, may, in fact, be something nineteen children will find absolutely boring!

- The teacher's role is a facilitator of problem-solving activities rather than a giver of knowledge.
- Students are constantly busy, actively engaging in learning activities.
- Learning and growth (the desire to know) come from within the child.
- Children develop naturally, and they will learn what is meaningful to them when they are biologically (physically) ready to learn.

You know about the **traditional classroom,** but what will you see in a **developmentally appropriate, child-centered classroom?** You will see:

- a large group meeting area, usually brightly colored carpet, where students engage in group discussions, interactions with the teacher and the assistant teacher, and informal exchanges of ideas.
- small group work areas, readied with necessary materials and tools, where students share, plan, and learn together.

- large display boards and tables where students exhibit their work products.
- storage spaces easily accessible to the students for personal belongings and for classroom materials and supplies.
- tables, chairs, beanbags, a reading loft, a sofa, a recliner, bookcases, file cabinets, and file boxes suited to the physical size and comfort of the students and classroom windows with colorful curtains or window shades.
- assortments of baskets, buckets, stacking boxes and bins, shoe bags, and clothes-lines.
- desks and chairs for the teacher and the assistant teacher located in obscure corners of the room.
- computer centers, writing and publishing centers, art and music centers, sand and water centers, math and science centers, social living and cooking centers, televisions, VCRs, cassette tape libraries, overhead transparency machines, and Big Book and regular-size book in-class libraries.

Simply stated, the **traditional** classroom radiates an atmosphere of the **teacher** as the **giver of knowledge**; whereas, the **child-centered, developmentally appropriate classroom** radiates an atmosphere of the **teacher** as the **facilitator of learning** - a move from the sometimes drab school-room to a colorful, warm, stimulating, inviting workplace environment.

Please keep in mind some schools and school districts do have more money than others and some teachers are more financially able than others to spend their own money on materials and supplies for the classroom. Just know wherever you are assigned, your teacher and the principal are probably doing all they possibly can to financially provide the best learning environment for the students.

**You must not,
nor do you have the right to,
criticize the furnishings
of the classroom.**

You **can** offer your time and talents
in painting, making curtains, donating
items, and many other low-cost or no-cost
services to ease your teacher's
already heavy burden of responsibilities.

YOUR TURN

(TWO PARTS)
PART I

DISCUSS WITH YOUR TEACHER HOW HE/SHE
INCORPORATES TRADITIONAL AND
DEVELOPMENTALLY APPROPRIATE
PRACTICES IN THE CLASSROOM. MAKE
NOTES IN THE SPACE PROVIDED.

_____

_____

_____

_____

_____

_____

_____

_____

_____

_____

_____

_____

_____

PART II

YOU AND YOUR TEACHER READ "HOW DO
CHILDREN LEARN MOST EFFECTIVELY?"
THEN ASK YOUR TEACHER TO COMMENT.
WRITE COMMENTS IN THE SPACE PROVIDED.

HOW DO CHILDREN LEARN MOST EFFECTIVELY?

WE ONCE THOUGHT CHILDREN LEARNED BEST WHEN THEY:
- LISTENED TO AND WATCHED ADULTS
- MEMORIZED FACTS
- THOUGHT ABOUT ABSTRACT IDEAS
- FOLLOWED DIRECTIONS
- HAD THEIR MISTAKES CORRECTED
- PRACTICED TASKS SELECTED BY OTHERS
- SAT QUIETLY AT DESKS

NOW WE KNOW CHILDREN LEARN BEST WHEN THEY:
- ACTIVELY PARTICIPATE
- WORK AT THEIR OWN PACE AND IN THEIR OWN STYLE
- TALK WITH EACH OTHER
- USE REAL OBJECTS AS PART OF THEIR LEARNING
- BUILD ON THEIR OWN EXPERIENCES
- FOLLOW THEIR NATURAL CURIOSITY
- EXPERIMENT TO FIND SOLUTIONS TO THEIR OWN REAL PROBLEMS
- CHOOSE WHAT THEY WANT TO LEARN, WITHIN REASON
- PLAY

CHAPTER 9

What Do School Administrators, Principals and Teachers Mean When They Say . . . ? Are You Still Confused?

Let's explore the **what-izzes**. Many authors write about these **what-izzes**. Every author takes a little different twist and slant, but the concepts are basically the same.

What is whole language?

Whole language is a way of thinking about language. Reading, writing, listening, and speaking are equally important functions of our language. Whole language teachers know this and plan for their students to be actively engaged in these functions.

Beverly Eisele, author of *Managing the Whole Language Classroom*, states, "Whole language is not a thing, it is not a set of materials, and it is not a prescription for success. Whole language is a way of thinking about how children learn language - oral and written language.

"Children naturally acquire oral language by listening and talking. During these (preschool) developing years perfection is not expected; children are free to make mistakes and approximations. Adults are understanding and accepting because they realize that learning language takes time and practice.

"However, when children begin to read and write (in school and at home), immediate success is often expected. As with oral language, children need ample time to practice reading and writing through meaningful experiences. They also need the freedom to make mistakes. Because whole language teachers understand how children learn language, they provide time and practical learning opportunities for literacy development."

In Ken Goodman's book *What's Whole in Whole Language?* he gives us a vivid picture of what whole language is **not**.

"Whole language firmly rejects such things as these:

- isolating skill (reading, language, phonics, spelling) sequences (in the learning/teaching process).
- slicing up reading and writing into grade slices (levels), each slice neatly following and dependent on prior ones.

- simplifying texts by controlling their sentence structures and vocabulary, or organizing them around phonic patterns (basal readers).
- equating reading and writing with scores on tests of 'subskills'.
- isolating reading and writing instruction from its use in learning, or in actual reading and writing.
- believing there are substantial numbers of learners who have difficulty learning to read or write for any physical or intellectual reason."

Here is another example of what whole language is **not**. Remember when you were in school and everyone in the classroom was instructed to "Get out your book and turn to page 435. Read pages 435 through 467. Answer the five questions on page 467 in complete sentences."

- Remember? -

Now, let me ask you some questions.

- Was it necessary that everyone get out a particular book and turn to the same page, read the same number of pages, and answer the same five questions?
- Did you need the information on those pages?
- How did you answer those five questions? Did you find the answer as quickly as you could in the text and copy the answer almost word for word?
- Do you remember today what you read back then? Do you remember the questions? Do you remember the answers to those questions?

See!

You did not learn anything!

Perhaps many of you experienced a whole language learning situation as a young person. Let's look at the following example.

One day your father came home from work and asked if you would like to go on a family vacation during the summer. You were excited beyond belief. He told you he had received information from three vacation spots and you could choose which one. He also told you the literature packets were on the dining room table. What did you do? You ran to the dining room table, grabbed the packets, tore them open as quickly as you could, and immediately started devouring the pictures and the words. If you came to a word that you did not recognize, you either skipped it or asked your father or mother. You called your seven best friends. You called your grandmother in Wisconsin. You called your aunt in San Francisco. You stood in the teachers' parking lot the next morning anxiously waiting for your teacher to arrive. You just had to tell her. You asked her to help you find all the information possible on your chosen site. You read the encyclopedia and all materials available in the school library. You were totally prepared for your summer vacation!

- Remember? -

Now, let me ask you some more questions.

- Were you excited about your reading assignment?
- Did you need to know the information?
- Did anyone tell you how much or how little to read?
- Did you want to tell others?
- Do you remember to this day the reading experience?
- Do you still want to share this story?

**That, my friends,
is
whole language.**

Whole language teachers **do not** have to throw out or burn basal readers and their accompanying teachers' guides. They do not have to let dust collect on reading workbooks or skills sheets. They **must**, however, view these marketed packages as one of many tools for learning to read in the classroom.

The whole language teacher provides a print-rich environment for authentic reading in the

 classroom. Posters, maps, paperback books (trade books) that interest **all** students, Big Books, regular hardback books, books on tape, sentence strips and markers, stacks and stacks of writing paper and pencils, old magazines and catalogs, colors, paints, glue, scissors, tape, bookbinding equipment, and all other tools necessary for the reading-writing process are readily available to students.

**True whole language teachers
do teach
reading strategies, skills, phonics, and spelling -
but - through literature choices appropriate for
each child guided by specific needs of the child.**

True whole language teachers model literacy behaviors for students. They advocate Sustained Silent Reading, a time-block during the day when everyone, including adults, reads just for the pleasure of reading. They support Journal Writing Time, a time-block during the day when everyone, including adults, writes in his/her personal journal.

They promote reading to students during a set time every day. They invite other students and school personnel, parents, and community leaders into their classrooms to read to the students.

They encourage their students to engage in meaningful conversations. Yes, that does mean **talking in the classroom.** Most of all, they show by their actions that reading, writing, listening, and speaking are wonderful and exciting ways to communicate.

What is a portfolio?

A portfolio is a continuous collection of a student's work samples and information documenting that student's progress. The student, the teacher, and the assistant teacher work together to develop the portfolio. From a portfolio all three persons know where the student has been, where the student is now, and a sense of where the student is going. **Planned conference time with each student is essential.** Very interesting and revealing dialogue results when students talk about their work.

What is a portfolio? A portfolio is a visual presentation of the student's capabilities, strengths, weaknesses, accomplishments, and progress.

Please **do not** confuse a portfolio with the traditional take-home folder. **They are not the same.** The student directs the content of the portfolio; whereas, the teacher decides the content of the traditional take-home folder.

What is portfolio assessment?

When you were in school, tests were probably the most used tools for evaluating your progress. When a test was returned there were check marks on the paper for the items missed. The total number of "misses" was multiplied by some number. The product was then subtracted from 100 and you received a number grade that was converted to an A, B, C, D, and, perish the thought, an F. **And that was that!**

Today when portfolios are used as the primary tool for assessing a student's growth and progress, a completely new mind-set is established. Listen to what Janine Batzle, author of *Portfolio Assessment and Evaluation*, has to say.

- "We see what children are doing rather than what they are not doing.

- We understand children learn and progress developmentally and uniquely, not by grade level.
- Assessment and evaluation match instruction in the classroom, with the teacher and student as the primary evaluators.
- The progress of a child is documented over time and based upon a variety of evidence rather than on a test.
- We find other ways to show growth rather than rely on numerical summaries."

The beauty of using the student portfolio for assessment and evaluation is the acceptance and appreciation of **each** child as a unique individual. When the teacher compares Leighton to Bob to Jamal to Sally to Zantunna to Nao to Elizabeth by using test grades **only - every child eventually loses!**

Please hear me out. Tests are not inherently bad. Test grades **are damaging when they are used habitually to label students, to group students, and to stigmatize students. (Remember the red birds, the blue birds, and the turtles?)**

What you will probably see in the elementary school classrooms are teachers who use a combination of the portfolio assessment and test grades to establish a **learning profile** for each student.

What is cooperative learning?

Cooperative learning is nothing new; however, its importance has long been overlooked as a necessary component of good instructional practice in the classroom. The essentials of cooperation are witnessed every day outside the classroom in recess games children play: jump rope, Duck Duck Goose, tug-of-war, and for older students, theater productions, band concerts, and football games, to name only a few.

What **is** cooperative learning? It is learning that takes place as the result of two or more people working together toward a common goal with positive interaction between the people involved.

Yes, there is a place for individualized learning in the elementary school classroom. There are many times when students want to learn on their own and activities must be provided for each student to excel. There is nothing more rewarding than hearing a child exclaim, **"Wow, I really did this myself!"**

Today most elementary classroom teachers also plan for cooperative learning experiences.

Why? Research and experience show that cooperative learning has advantages for intellectual development and for social development. Authors Susan and Tim Hill explain these advantages in *The Collaborative Classroom*.

"Through social interaction:

- higher achievement is evident.
- deeper levels of understanding form.
- enjoyable learning experiences result.
- leadership skills develop.
- positive attitudes are nurtured.
- high self-esteem thrives.
- all students are included in the learning process.
- a sense of belonging exists.
- future, workplace skills are developed."

Do elementary school children know how to work together cooperatively? **No.** This behavior has to be taught. Effective classroom teachers **plan** on teaching these behaviors to the students. This teaching is not a one-time affair. Especially for younger students, rules and procedures for cooperative learning experiences **must** be gone over daily. The more students experience group success, the more they will be reinforced to focus on a common goal and to value the presence of other individuals in the group. Your job, as the elementary classroom assistant teacher, is to support the classroom teacher in this undertaking. At first, you and she/he will wonder if **any** good could possibly surface through the chaos and confusion. Have patience and you **will** see the rewards are well worth the effort.

Some elementary teachers use competitive, in-class instructional activities. Games played in the classroom are not necessarily cooperative learning experiences. Used in moderation, these activities are exciting and stimulating, but if used to the excess, the teacher is sending out a clear message that only a few students are capable of achieving.

Remember the weekly Spelling Bees or the daily Multiplication-Facts-Quick-Drills? Letonia always won the Spelling Bee and Samuel always won the Quick Drill. And where was Diane? She was probably sitting at her desk with her coat over her head trying to hide embarrassment.

**She absolutely hated
Letonia and Samuel!
She hated the teacher
for allowing those two activities!**

What are learning centers?

A learning center is any part of the classroom designated for **independent** learning. Do not mistake learning center activities with fun activities planned by the teacher for all students after the day's work is completed.

 Learning centers are **fun**.

Learning centers are **activities**.

Learning centers are **planned by the teacher.**

Learning centers are **for all students.**

Now, get ready for the
big difference.

Learning centers are developed by the teacher and the assistant teacher for specific, independent instruction.

Learning centers are used for **all** subject areas. The centers can be simple or complex. They can be expensive or inexpensive, but they **must** all be creative and inviting to the student. Each center **must** include the following:

- The Objective - "Why am I doing this activity?"
- Simple Directions - "How do I do this activity?"
- A Model (when appropriate) - "Could you give me an idea?"
- Materials - "What will I need?"
- A Self-Checking System - "I want to know if I have been successful without asking the teacher or the assistant."
- Follow-Up or Recognition - "Where do I go from here?" - or - "Yes, I get this certificate (sticker) to take home!"

Learning centers are an exciting alternative to the old, traditional seat work. Depending on the center, students are encouraged to work cooperatively or independently. However, to be truly effective for instruction, learning centers must be changed frequently. Reestablishing centers will, no doubt, be something that your teacher will ask **you** to do.

What are learning styles?

Think back on your school days. Did your mother ever furiously knock on your bedroom door demanding that you turn down the volume on your stereo while you did your homework? Did your father chide you for munching chocolate chip cookies as you prepared your book report? Did your grandmother exclaim how you were going blind in the next thirty-five seconds from reading in a dimly lit room?

Your family did what they thought was absolutely right for you at the time. Thank goodness you had a family who cared. However, researchers investigating how children learn have recently discovered **learning styles.** Learning styles have been around for as long as people have been around, but educators are just now beginning to see their place in the instructional program of the elementary school classroom.

Rita and Kenneth Dunn and Marie Carbo are three leading learning styles researchers. This is what they have to say. "Everyone has a learning style. You have one, and so does your spouse if you are married. Your children have one too - both your biological offspring and the ones you teach. People's styles determine how they begin to concentrate every time they have new or difficult knowledge or skills to master.

"Every one has a learning style, but each person's is different - like fingerprints. Fingerprints are similar in many ways, but specialists trained to tell the differences can identify which belong to whom. Learning style specialists can do even more than diagnose and match styles; they can describe how to learn more with less effort and remember better than ever before, merely by capitalizing on each individual's unique characteristics.

"Learning style is the way that students of every age (adults, too) are affected by their:

- immediate environment
- own emotions
- sociological needs
- physical characteristics
- psychological inclinations

when concentrating and trying to master and remember new or difficult information or skills.

Children learn best
only
when they use their learning style characteristics
advantageously; otherwise they study,
but
often forget what they tried to learn."

Wait!

Do not put the book down!

Marie Carbo and Rita and Kenneth Dunn have given us more information to explain learning style characteristics. They use the term "elements" to describe conditions that bombard us every single moment.

Sound, light, temperature, and room arrangement affect us in many ways. What is comfortable to one person is a distracter to another.

Our emotional makeup must be considered, also. How are we motivated and for how long? Are we persistent or do we give up easily? How responsible are we? Do we work best in structured situations, or does structure bother us?

Look at how you prefer to work. Do you like to work by yourself? Do you work well paired with another person or as part of a team?

Physical elements are important, too. Your five senses, seeing, tasting, hearing, touching, and smelling, are a critical part of your learning style. Again, what bothers one person, is of no consequence to another. Do you like to eat while you learn? Do you like to have a cup of coffee while you are reading a difficult document such as the deed to your new house? Is there a certain time of day that is more conducive to learning for you? Do you learn better sitting down or moving about?

You can readily see all of the things (elements) that affect **how we learn.**

Many elementary school teachers know about learning styles, have run learning styles inventories on their students, and are using these inventories to enable **each student to learn more and to learn better.** Be prepared to see some unusual classroom events. Keith and Brighton are eating popcorn while they work their math problems. MaLei is cuddling a fuzzy teddy bear as she writes her story. Markus is under the table reading his library book. Juan is talking to himself as he puts a puzzle together. Daniel is waiting for you to tell him to get started on his work.

"**Crazy!**" you say.

No, **learning styles!**

What is this new grouping?

You are referring to Multiage Grouping, or as sometimes called, Multilevel Grouping. This concept goes back to pioneer days in America. Basically, it is "The Little Red Schoolhouse" idea. One school marm taught children of all ages all subjects in one little room.

Over the years, American educators decided children should be taught in grades, based primarily on chronological age. **One grade level equals one physical growth year of the child.** If the child learns what is taught in one grade, then the child is promoted to the next grade. If the child does not learn what is prescribed in one grade, then the child fails. Life is nice for kids who fit into just this plan, but the poor kid who needs a few more months to learn is labeled as slow, dumb, or stupid. Or, what is to be done with that smarty kid who learns everything that one grade has to offer in the first two months of school and wants to move to the next grade? School administrators are still trying to find an answer to that question. And yes, elementary school children are, for the most part, still placed in graded learning blocks - The Grade Trap.

However, in their search, educators now suggest the pioneer model has much to offer. True, elementary school teachers no longer haul wood to make fires, wear long dresses, or put their hair in buns, but they are being allowed to investigate the many benefits of teaching students of mixed ages.

Please allow me to insert a personal story.

The Benefits of Multiage Grouping

My formal education began in the early 1950s in rural north Mississippi. The little country school housed six grades, seven counting Primer. Primer, Grades One and Two had one teacher. Grades Three and Four had one teacher. Grades Five and Six had one teacher who also served as the principal. Many days we were one large group, especially if one or two teachers were absent. Electricity, running water, and indoor facilities were ours, but that was about it. We were of necessity a **family of learners.** We really had no other choice.

Were we smart? **Yes!**
Did we learn? **Yes!**

What did we learn?

We learned the **five Rs!**

- Reading
- Writing ('riting)
- Arithmetic ('rithmetic)
- **Respect**
- **Responsibility**

I quickly learned that James Ferris, a fifth grader, was a powerful leader. Attila the Hun had to have been his distant relative. His self-appointed job was to make us little kids line up outside and march into the school every morning. If we had mud on our shoes, James Ferris quickly chastised us on the spot. We were instructed to take off the shoes, go to the back of the line, and wait until he could personally escort us to the principal to offer a thousand apologies for our indiscretion. One day I mustered enough courage to give James Ferris a banana. He looked somewhat puzzled, said a quick "Thanks," and turned his back on me in a flash. We were all amazed when James Ferris played Frosty the Snowman in our Christmas pageant. He bounced and sang his way across the tiny stage. He was truly a jolly soul. When we returned from the holiday, James Ferris was once again the drill sergeant.

My second-grade job, which I took quite seriously, was to hold Shirley in an upright position when she went to the bathroom. Shirley was an adorable Primer child, but she either fell in the toilet, soaked her dress sash, or came out of the bathroom with the tail of her dress wrapped in her panties. Shirley wore a dress with a big sash every day. Her mother told her the devil would get her if she wore long-legged, corduroy britches.

By far the MVP (Most Valuable Player) Award went to Billy Neal. Billy Neal and his mother lived close to the school. He did not have to ride that horrible school bus. Billy Neal walked to school. His job was school gardener. He took excellent care of our garden year-round. We had peas, corn, tomatoes, butter beans, okra, watermelons, and cantaloupes. Billy Neal assigned every student in the whole school garden jobs. In addition to preparing the succulent vegetables, our one cook made huge pans of cornbread and large jars of sweet tea for her special contribution.

I absolutely lived for the day when I would graduate from pea sheller to butter bean sheller. You see, Billy Neal had this formula figured out. Graduating to butter bean sheller was only accomplished if you could shell a big, long, purple hull pea in the time it took him to pick up twenty gravel rocks. I'm talking about quality shelling, too. Each pea had to be perfectly clean and perfectly separate from the other peas. If a worm happened to be thrown in, you were immediately disqualified.

One day Billy Neal did not come to school. He didn't come the next day either, nor the next. I overheard my grandmother talking to one of her friends. "Maude, it's just going to be better on all the family. They told her she could go to see him four times a year."

No one said a word. Grass grew taller and taller in the garden. I never graduated to butter bean sheller.

Years later I learned Billy Neal died in a mental institution. He was called a Mongolian idiot. Now we know Billy Neal had Down's syndrome. When I learned of his death, my heart broke.

Every life should be blessed with a James Ferris, a Shirley, and a Billy Neal.

Need I say more?

What are the Math (NCTM) Standards?

When teachers discuss teaching mathematics to the "Standards" they are referring to standards written by the National Council of Teachers of Mathematics. This lengthy document (1989) established national expectations for teaching and evaluating mathematics in Kindergarten through Grade 12.

Stop!
Think for just a minute.

When is the **only** time you really need to know math? And, the answer is - **When you have a problem to solve!** "How much interest will I pay if I borrow money to buy a new car?" "Should I double or triple the recipe to have enough chicken casserole to feed my guests?"

Elementary school children rattle off math facts like clockwork; however, when they come to the sections in the math book on problem solving, they go completely blank. Why? First, math book word problems are basically not appropriate or meaningful in their lives. Second, they have not been taught the relationship between numbers and words. Did I say words? Yes. The NCTM Standards stress mathematical literacy. How does this work?

Students still need to know the facts, but they need to know so much more. Here are the five general NCTM goals for students.

- Students will learn to value mathematics.
- Students will become confident in their ability to do mathematics.
- Students will become mathematical problem solvers.
- Students will learn to communicate mathematically.
- Students will learn to reason mathematically.

To accomplish these goals at all grade levels, students must be allowed to read, write, and discuss, **yes, talk about** mathematics. Students **must** have manipulatives (fraction pieces, unit cubes, base-10 blocks, etc.) to construct mathematical situations. They should be encouraged to explore, to guess (make approximations), to make errors, and to correct those errors. By doing these things, they will become more and more confident in their ability to do math.

Once again, teachers should **not** throw out the math textbooks. They should, however, think of the math book as only one teaching tool.

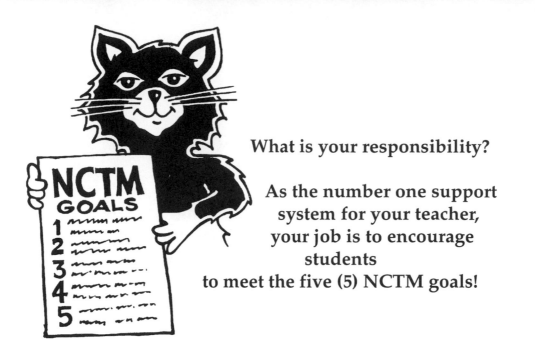

What is your responsibility?

As the number one support system for your teacher, your job is to encourage students to meet the five (5) NCTM goals!

Is everything hands-on in Science and Social Studies?

Yes, and this is **especially** true for Science and Social Studies. For years experts have argued which is more important, the content or the process. The answer is quite simple - **both.** The key is for students to learn the content of Science and Social Studies through inquiry and discovery. Good teachers know the art of balancing the two. If content is stressed too much, then "Why do we have to do this boring stuff?" is heard. If process is overstressed, then students have a great time experimenting, but they will not be able to tell you one thing that they learned.

Just like Math, Science and Social Studies must be meaningful. Isn't it more important for elementary school students to investigate how rock formations and land elevation affected the lives of the Native American Indians who once lived in their area than to memorize a twenty-item list of generic rock facts they will soon forget?

I hope by now you are asking, "If **everything** elementary school students need to know is connected, how in the world can this information be separated into different subjects?"

Good for you!

You are exactly right!

Information students **need** to know cannot be separated.

That brings us to the last **what-izz** in this chapter.

What are thematic units?
Is this how teachers integrate the curriculum?

A thematic unit is a system of organizing instructional time and materials around a topic that lends itself to the integration (combination) of all subjects. Combining these subjects into multi-purpose lessons is not a new idea. However, there is renewed interest in this instructional strategy as research confirms its tremendous benefits.

Let's look at the development of a thematic unit. This model is one example of thematic unit development. Many times the teacher in a self-contained classroom develops and teaches a unit with assistance only from **you.**

Our Fifty States

Mrs. Devon, Miss Shores, and Mr. Holland are fifth-grade teachers at Monument Elementary School. Mrs. Devon teaches Language Arts, Miss Shores teaches Math and Science, and Mr. Holland teaches Social Studies and a combination of Art/Music. All three teachers were bored using the state-adopted textbooks day in and day out and so were their students. They had heard of thematic unit development, but they were not quite sure how to begin. Miss Shores telephoned a friend who taught in another elementary school seeking her guidance. Miss Kellerman promised to meet with the three Monument Elementary teachers the following Thursday afternoon during their planning time.

Step I

Miss Kellerman asked each teacher to focus on the particular subject(s) he/she taught and brainstorm ideas and activities that could be used in a study of the fifty states. They were also asked to keep in mind the state-mandated curriculum objectives for teaching the fifty states.

Step II

She asked the three teachers to complete a form similar to Beverly Eisele's model in *Managing the Whole Language Classroom*. (See Eisele Model on adjacent page.)

Step III

Excitement begot excitement! Soon all three teachers compiled an extremely long list of thrilling experiences for the students - all constructed around the theme Our Fifty States.

Step IV

Mrs. Devon, Miss Shores, and Mr. Holland discussed at great length **how** their thoughts should be written as instructional objectives.

Thematic Unit Development

Managing the Whole Language Classroom (CTP 3220) © 1991
Printed with permission from Creative Teaching Press, Inc.,
15342 Graham Street, Huntington Beach, CA 92649-1111.

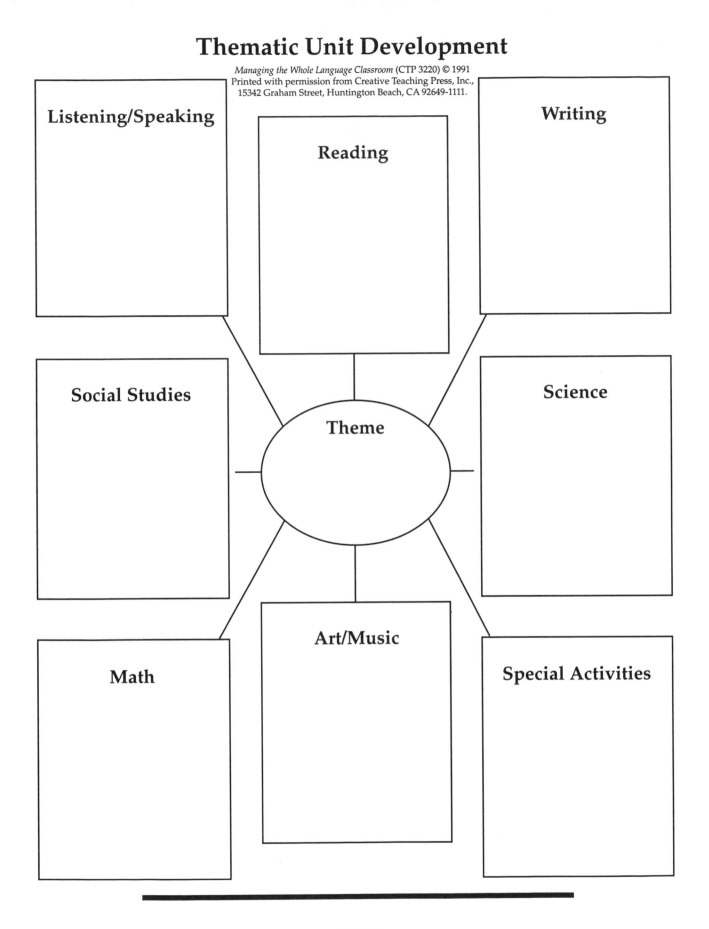

Listening/Speaking

Reading

Writing

Social Studies

Theme

Science

Math

Art/Music

Special Activities

Step V

They wrote each objective **cooperatively.** Yes, they worked just like students in cooperative learning groups.

Step VI

Then another important question arose.

Would they teach the thematic unit using time blocks already established for their subjects?

- or -

Would they ask the principal if they could use the gymnasium and have all fifth graders working together in one long time-block?

They decided to use the gym.

Step VII

All three teachers started preparing for the unit presentation.

Time passed.

Miss Kellerman was invited to see "The Nifty Fifty," a play written and produced by the fifth graders at Monument Elementary. She also learned that during the past five weeks:

- There had been no behavior problems. All students had been totally engaged in their learning.
- Mrs. Devon had guided the students in reading library books about the fifty states. She had helped the students write and illustrate their own class book, *Malcolm the Martian Visits America*.
- Miss Shores had coached the students in writing their own math/science book, which included planning and budgeting money for a trip from Denver, Colorado, to Washington, D.C. Also, comparative charts and graphs showing weather information

from all fifty states lined the fifth grade halls.

- Mr. Holland had helped the students construct an 18' x 32' relief map of the United States. Junk sculptures representing each state had been made by designated student groups.
- Throughout the unit, mothers of fifth graders had prepared foods from different sections of the country for tasting parties.
- Local newspaper reporters and television camera crews had come to Monument Elementary throughout the thematic unit. The students had posed for pictures and had given interviews. They were stars!

"Wait just a minute!"

"Are you telling me all of this happened because three teachers decided to teach thematically?"

Yes!

Guess what else happened?

The principal of Monument Elementary School
had to call substitute teachers
for
Mrs. Devon, Miss Shores, and Mr. Holland
the day after the end-of-the-unit play!

Why?

**They were granted personal leave
because
they were completely exhausted!**

Why should teachers use thematic units?

- Students learn **best** when subjects are integrated.
- Themes allow skills to be taught through activities and projects that relate to **real life experiences.**
- Themes help direct long- and short-range goals.
- Themes may be changed to fit the needs of students from year to year.

Elementary classroom teachers know planning thematic units takes **time.** Picking up a Teacher's Guide in a particular subject and rapidly hurling information at twenty-eight students is so much easier. However, teachers who **"grab and teach"** never really see that spark in children when they know a thematic unit has been custom-made for them.

———

Whew!

That was by far the l-o-n-g-e-s-t chapter I have ever read in my whole, entire life!

YOUR TURN

THERE ARE MANY MORE **WHAT-IZZES**. BY NO MEANS HAVE WE COVERED ALL OF THEM. CHOOSE ONE FROM THE FOLLOWING LIST. ASK YOUR TEACHER ABOUT IT. THIS COULD BE SOMETHING THAT THE TWO OF YOU RESEARCH TOGETHER. ON THE LINES PROVIDED AFTER THE LIST, WRITE YOUR THOUGHTS AND COMMENTS.

THE LIST

1. HOWARD GARDNER'S MULTIPLE INTELLIGENCES
2. ROBERT STERNBERG'S QUESTIONING TECHNIQUES
3. BENJAMIN BLOOM'S TAXONOMY
4. INVENTED (INVENTIVE) SPELLING
5. INCLUSION
6. OUTCOME-BASED EDUCATION (OBE)
7. BRIAN CAMBOURNE'S SEVEN CONDITIONS THAT PROMOTE LANGUAGE ACQUISITION
9. WILLIAM GLASSER'S REALITY THERAPY
10. GRAPHIC ORGANIZERS
11. D. H. GRAVES - PROCESS WRITING

_____

_____

_____

CHAPTER 10

Look How Much You Know!

Chapter 10 is not a long chapter.
- but -
Chapter 10 is **very important!**

Let's revisit what we said about your position in the first few pages of this book.

Who are you?

You are the main support system for the elementary classroom teacher!

- Remember? -

How much have you grown? Where are you now? **You are literally walking in your teacher's shadow!**

Please do not be overwhelmed with such a multitude of things to do and things to learn. As you grow through training and through years of service, you will become even more outstanding than you are today.

The best advice for the elementary classroom assistant teacher - the paraeducator - is **get, and keep, a sense of humor.** You'll **never** last without it!

YOUR TURN

WRITE ONE HUMOROUS (FUNNY) THING
THAT HAS HAPPENED IN YOUR CLASSROOM.
WERE YOU ABLE TO LAUGH? I CERTAINLY
HOPE SO! SHARE YOUR STORY WITH
ANOTHER ASSISTANT. ASK THAT ASSISTANT
TO DO THE SAME.

_____

_____

_____

_____

_____

_____

_____

_____

_____

_____

_____

_____

_____

The next chapter is written for your teacher!

Take a well-deserved break!

See!

I told you chapter 10 would be short!

SECTION
TWO

STUDY GUIDE

SECTION TWO
STUDY GUIDE

CHAPTER 8:

1. Describe a typical **traditional** elementary school classroom.

2. Describe a typical **developmentally appropriate, child-centered** elementary school classroom.

3. List seven philosophy statements from the **teacher-centered (traditional) philosophy of Education.**

4. List eight philosophy statements from the **child-centered (developmentally appropriate) philosophy of Education.**

5. Discuss activities that occur in your classroom that are more **traditional.**

6. Discuss activities that occur in your classroom that are more **developmentally appropriate, child-centered.**

7. Compare and contrast how we once thought children learned best with how we know children learn best.

CHAPTER 9:

1. Briefly describe the following:

> Whole Language
> Portfolio/Portfolio Assessment
> Cooperative Learning
> Learning Centers
> Learning Styles
> Multiage/Multilevel Grouping
> Math (NCTM) Standards
> Hands-On Science and Social Studies
> Thematic Units
> Integrated Curriculum

2. Why should teachers use **thematic units?**

3. What is the **main reason** teachers are reluctant to teach thematically?

CHAPTER 10:

Why is having a **sense of humor** extremely important for the elementary classroom assistant teacher?

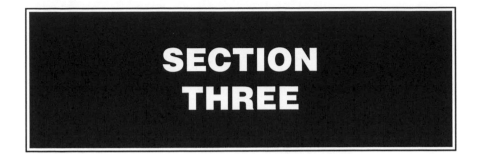

SECTION
THREE

CHAPTER 11

Just for the Classroom Teacher!

As an elementary classroom teacher working with an assistant, you are a leader of children - and adults. Many of you have had **no** training as managers of adults, especially adults who work so closely with you every day. Often your expectations are either too high or too low. You become frustrated when your assistant asks too many questions or when your assistant does not ask enough. You either give your assistant too much to do or you give your assistant too little. Am I being critical?

No, indeed.

You spent the majority of your college years preparing to teach children - **not adults.** You were the one being supervised.

Now you find yourself in a managerial role with never enough time or energy to train an assistant.
"If only I had more **time** to spend with him/her!"

Yes, you have said this often.

You are absolutely correct.

"What am **I** to do?" you ask.

Hopefully, I have made your job easier. By now, you are probably familiar with *The Paraeducator*, especially the **YOUR TURN** at the end of chapters 1 through 10.

**Thank you for contributing
your knowledge and your wisdom!**

Chapters 1 through 10 focus on such topics as:

- the assistant's job responsibilities
- the importance of communication
- the necessity of confidentiality
- current trends in Education

If you have not had the time to thoroughly peruse the book,

Go ahead!
Please do so **now!**

- Check the table of contents.
- Browse through the pages.
- Scan the evaluation forms.

Just as your assistant teacher is in the process of becoming effective in job expectations, you are in the process of becoming effective as a manager of the other adult in your classroom - **the elementary classroom assistant teacher.** How is this accomplished?

Carolyn Houk and Robert McKenzie, two prominent paraeducator team trainers, describe **good supervision.** "Good supervision doesn't just happen, but neither does it require extensive training on your part. In general, it calls for generous amounts of common sense, empathy, patience, and commitment from you. To provide quality supervision, you'll want to do the following:

- Establish and communicate to the assistant reasonable expectations for the job.
- Give the assistant a clear sense of his or her value in the classroom.
- Let the assistant know that you want to work in strong partnership together.
- Be readily available for consultation and help.
- Encourage initiative and creativity.

- Exhibit a professional attitude toward the assistant and model the behavior you expect.
- Try keeping the assistant's job from becoming static and routine.
- Urge the assistant to expand job-related knowledge and skills.
- Know when the assistant needs assurance and reinforcement.
- Make it a point to provide feedback in some way every day.
- View supervision as a continual and ongoing process."

A

very

important

and

specific

reminder

follows.

At the very beginning of the school year - the first parents' meeting, Open House, PTO, and via newsletter - introduce your paraeducator (assistant). Talk to your assistant beforehand concerning the introduction. If the principal has already made a general introduction of faculty and staff, go into more detail with the parents.

**Now
is the time to inform parents about:**

1. **what the assistant can do**
2. **what the assistant cannot do**
3. **treating the assistant with respect**

Parents are often confused about the role the assistant plays in the classroom. The responsibility of informing the parents is yours.

**Start the year off positively
for
the parents
and for
your assistant
by
taking the time to communicate
your
expectations!**

- Remember -

There will be times when you are extremely annoyed by either something your assistant says or does. Do not, I repeat, **do not** take the conflict out of your classroom! Use your conflict resolution skills to work through the problem with your assistant. Allow for your assistant having a "bad day" now and then, too.

Also, remember that approximately 98 percent of all assistants want to know and learn and grow professionally. However, approximately 2 percent, for whatever reasons, do not need to be working with children in the classroom. Hopefully that 2 percent have already recognized themselves in the preceding chapters. As you are well aware, some adults simply do not have the temperament to work with children every day.

Have patience with your assistant.

Keep a sense of humor!

You already know the importance of planning for your students. Planning for your assistant is equally important. For each objective think:

- What will **I** do?
- What will **my students** do?
- What will **my assistant** do?

There are jobs you will want your assistant to do year-round; however, there are jobs that will vary depending on your long-range instructional plan. Please complete the following Needs Survey. You have my permission to make copies of the Needs Survey. This instrument may be used in many ways - for each thematic unit, grading period, or instructional block - **you decide.**

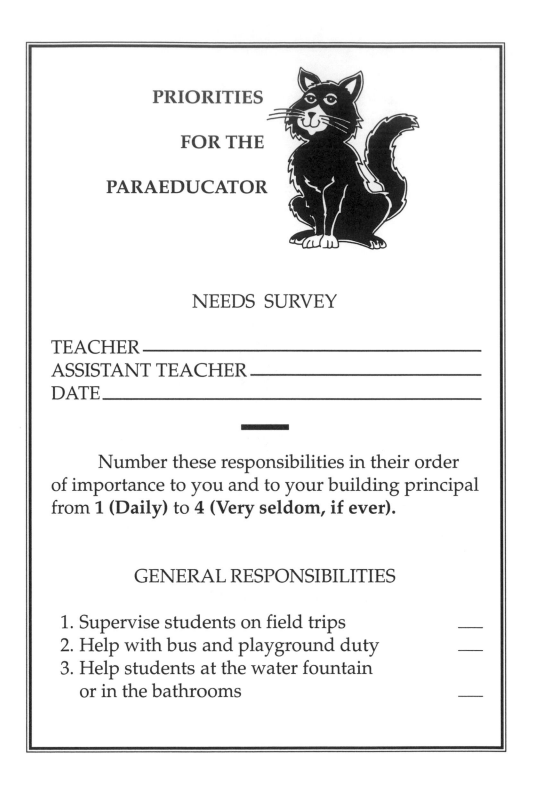

PRIORITIES

FOR THE

PARAEDUCATOR

NEEDS SURVEY

TEACHER————————————————
ASSISTANT TEACHER————————————
DATE————————————————————

———

    Number these responsibilities in their order of importance to you and to your building principal from **1 (Daily)** to **4 (Very seldom, if ever).**

GENERAL RESPONSIBILITIES

1. Supervise students on field trips   ——
2. Help with bus and playground duty   ——
3. Help students at the water fountain
   or in the bathrooms   ——

4. Supervise students in the cafeteria —

5. Help students with classroom housekeeping —

6. Supervise rest periods for students —

7. Weigh and measure students —

8. Assist students in the media center or in the computer lab —

9. Help students publish and display their work —

10. Assist students with project work —

11. Help prepare and decorate for programs or special events —

12. Attend parent-teacher conferences —

13. Care for younger brothers and sisters during parent-teacher conference —

14. Assist in caring for sick or injured students —

15. Ready materials and equipment for lessons and store materials after lessons —

16. Set up learning centers, cooking activities, science experiments, etc. —

17. Mix paints and wash brushes for the art center —

18. Make minor room repairs —

19. Help students care for inside pets —

20. Help put the room in order at the end of the day and ready the room for the next day —

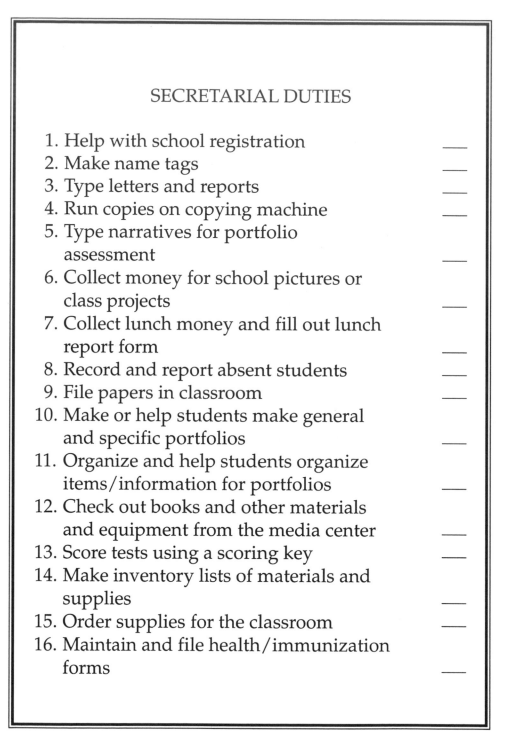

SECRETARIAL DUTIES

1. Help with school registration _____
2. Make name tags _____
3. Type letters and reports _____
4. Run copies on copying machine _____
5. Type narratives for portfolio assessment _____
6. Collect money for school pictures or class projects _____
7. Collect lunch money and fill out lunch report form _____
8. Record and report absent students _____
9. File papers in classroom _____
10. Make or help students make general and specific portfolios _____
11. Organize and help students organize items/information for portfolios _____
12. Check out books and other materials and equipment from the media center _____
13. Score tests using a scoring key _____
14. Make inventory lists of materials and supplies _____
15. Order supplies for the classroom _____
16. Maintain and file health/immunization forms _____

17. Take notes during teacher-planning meetings ___
18. Collect and organize materials for thematic units ___
19. Send notes home to parents ___
20. Collect forms sent from home ___
21. Telephone parents or guardians of children who are absent ___
22. Telephone parents or guardians to verify student information ___
23. Telephone parents or guardians to remind them of conferences or meetings ___

INSTRUCTIONAL RESPONSIBILITIES

1. Work with small groups in activities that have been initiated by you ___
2. Assist with large group, instructional activities ___
3. Assist with makeup work ___
4. Assist with work and activities for students needing extra help ___
5. Read or tell stories to students ___
6. Listen to students read ___
7. Write for students as they dictate their stories ___

8. Teach songs, games, and finger-plays ___
9. Assist with art activities ___
10. Help with daily, weekly, and long-range instructional planning ___
11. Prepare instructional materials ___
12. Participate in informing parents/guardians of instructional progress of students ___
13. Supply information in evaluating students' portfolios ___
14. Help plan project work ___
15. Help collect materials for project work ___
16. Help organize materials for project work ___

OTHER
JOBS

_____

_____
_____
_____
_____
_____
_____
_____
_____
_____
_____
_____

Share the Needs Survey with your assistant.

Are you expecting too much?

Are you expecting too little?

The two of you decide!

––––––––––––––––––––

Please, please, remember,
if your assistant is inexperienced,
ask him/her to gradually accept
more and more
responsibilities
- and -
offer lots of praise and encouragement.

Chapter 12 is for **your assistant** and for **you**, too. After both of you have read chapter 12, if you have not done so already, establish a daily, weekly, and/or monthly planning time with your assistant. Also, make a schedule for **formal** assessment and evaluation.

**Be sure to share these ideas
with your principal.**

Do not forget the importance
of
informal assessment and evaluation.

CHAPTER 12

Reflection Time for You -
the Paraeducator
in the Elementary School Classroom!

Now you realize how
very important you are!

Road Map for Success

"How am I progressing?"
you ask.

Your First Stop: General
Self-Evaluation

You know better than anyone!

Self-evaluation is possibly the best tool to measure growth. Please read each item on the following form carefully and mark the answer that **best** describes you. You have my permission to make copies of all evaluation forms in this chapter.

Be honest, but do not be too hard on yourself. There are always areas that need improving.

THE PARAEDUCATOR

-

THE ELEMENTARY CLASSROOM
ASSISTANT TEACHER

-

SELF-EVALUATION

_____

ASSISTANT TEACHER _____
TEACHER _____
DATE _____

Directions: For each item, circle the rating that **BEST** describes you. Space is provided for additional comments.

Always   Sometimes   Rarely   Never
Not Applicable

INSTRUCTION

1. I can evaluate how much a student already knows about a certain subject.   A   S   R   N   NA

2. I explain a lesson's objective clearly.   A   S   R   N   NA

3. I give easily understood directions and instructions.   A   S   R   N   NA

4. I focus on the lesson's objective.   A   S   R   N   NA

5. I present a lesson in a creative and interesting way.   A   S   R   N   NA

6. I regularly check for students' understanding.   A   S   R   N   NA

7. I pace a lesson based on the students' rates of learning.   A   S   R   N   NA

8. I provide examples and models when they are needed in a lesson.   A   S   R   N   NA

9. I ask questions that call for more than yes/no answers or one-word answers. A S R N NA

10. I provide assistance to students when they need help during practice sessions. A S R N NA

11. I monitor students during independent practice sessions. A S R N NA

12. I plan on reviewing with students who need extra review. A S R N NA

13. I understand the difficulty of lesson material. A S R N NA

14. I understand the needs and the abilities of all students. A S R N NA

15. I provide "hands-on" learning activities for students. A S R N NA

16. I readily admit when I do not know the answers to students' questions and I model appropriate learner behavior by researching the topic to find the answers. A S R N NA

CLASSROOM MANAGEMENT

1. I follow classroom routines. A S R N NA

2. I enforce classroom rules firmly and fairly. A S R N NA

3. I delegate routine tasks to students. A S R N NA

4. I understand and support discipline strategies in my building/district. A S R N NA

5. I use a pleasant tone of voice. A S R N NA

6. I understand and support cooperative learning activities. A S R N NA

7. I show no racial or sexual preference in my interaction with students. A   S   R   N   NA

8. I am well organized and I model this behavior for students. A   S   R   N   NA

9. I am flexible if the daily schedule is changed. A   S   R   N   NA

10. I am efficient in time management. A   S   R   N   NA

11. I exhibit little or no anxiety if left in charge of the classroom. A   S   R   N   NA

RELATIONSHIPS WITH STUDENTS

1. I treat students with courtesy and respect. A   S   R   N   NA

2. I communicate high expectations. A   S   R   N   NA

3. I model positive behaviors. A   S   R   N   NA

4. I ask for and accept ideas from students. A S R N NA

5. I offer specific and appropriate praise to students. A S R N NA

6. I motivate students to do their best work. A S R N NA

7. I promote realistic self-esteem in students. A S R N NA

8. I encourage responsibility. A S R N NA

9. I encourage independence. A S R N NA

10. I understand and acknowledge individual learning styles. A S R N NA

11. I listen to students without passing judgment on what is said. A S R N NA

12. I understand the necessity of confidentiality in what my students tell me. A S R N NA

ADDITIONAL COMMENTS

_____
_____
_____
_____
_____
_____
_____
_____
_____
_____
_____
_____
_____
_____
_____
_____
_____
_____
_____
_____
_____

ASSISTANT TEACHER'S SIGNATURE   TEACHER'S SIGNATURE

_____   _____

DATE   DATE

_____   _____

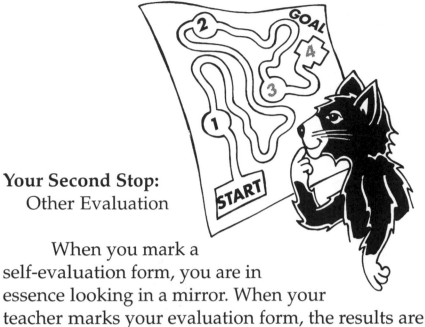

Your Second Stop:
Other Evaluation

When you mark a self-evaluation form, you are in essence looking in a mirror. When your teacher marks your evaluation form, the results are similar to photographs taken of you.

Ask your teacher to mark the following evaluation form. When the form is completed, share the information with each other. **Go over each item.** See how your responses are alike and how they are different.

You may not always agree, but do listen carefully to suggestions your teacher makes. Teachers do not have eyes in the back of their heads and if there are some items that need clarifying, please offer examples of how you have constructively addressed those concerns.

THE PARAEDUCATOR

-

THE ELEMENTARY CLASSROOM
ASSISTANT TEACHER

-

EVALUATION

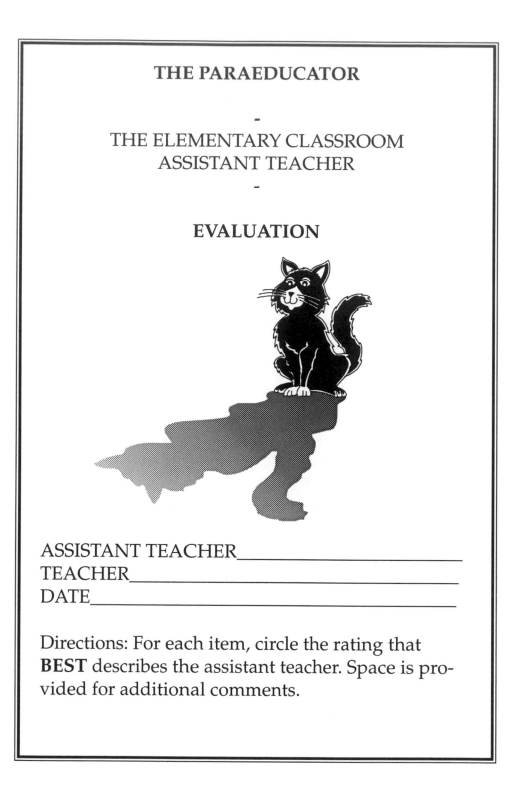

ASSISTANT TEACHER_____

TEACHER_____

DATE_____

Directions: For each item, circle the rating that
BEST describes the assistant teacher. Space is provided for additional comments.

MY ASSISTANT TEACHER:

**Always   Sometimes   Rarely   Never
Not Applicable**

INSTRUCTION

1. Evaluates how much a student already knows about a certain subject.   A S R N NA

2. Explains a lesson's objective clearly.   A S R N NA

3. Gives easily understood directions and instructions.   A S R N NA

4. Focuses on the lesson's objective.   A S R N NA

5. Presents lesson in a creative and interesting way.   A S R N NA

6. Regularly checks for students' understanding.   A S R N NA

7. Paces a lesson based on the
students' rates of learning. A S   R   N   NA

8. Provides examples and
models when needed.   A S   R   N   NA

9. Asks questions that call
for more than yes/no or
one-word answers -
(higher-order thinking
skills.)   A S   R   N   NA

10. Helps students willingly. A S   R   N   NA

11. Monitors independent
practice.   A S   R   N   NA

12. Plans for review.   A S   R   N   NA

13. Understands the difficulty
of lesson material.   A S   R   N   NA

14. Understands the needs
and the abilities of all
students.   A S   R   N   NA

15. Provides for "hands-on"
learning activities.   A S   R   N   NA

16. Admits not knowing answers but researches to find answers to those questions.   A   S   R   N   NA

CLASSROOM MANAGEMENT

1. Follows classroom routines.   A   S   R   N   NA

2. Enforces classroom rules firmly and fairly.   A   S   R   N   NA

3. Delegates routine tasks to students.   A   S   R   N   NA

4. Understands and supports discipline strategies for building/district.   A   S   R   N   NA

5. Uses a pleasant voice tone. A   S   R   N   NA

6. Understands and supports cooperative learning activities.   A   S   R   N   NA

7. Shows no racial or sexual preference in interactions with students.   A   S   R   N   NA

8. Is well organized and models organizational skills for students. A S R N NA

9. Is flexible if daily schedule is changed. A S R N NA

10. Is efficient in time management. A S R N NA

11. Exhibits little or no anxiety if left in charge of the classroom for short time periods. A S R N NA

RELATIONSHIP WITH STUDENTS

1. Treats students with courtesy and respect. A S R N NA

2. Communicates high expectations. A S R N NA

3. Models positive behaviors. A S R N NA

4. Asks for and accepts ideas from students. A S R N NA

5. Offers specific and
   appropriate praise.   A   S   R   N   NA

6. Motivates students to do
   their best work.   A   S   R   N   NA

7. Promotes realistic
   self-esteem in students.   A   S   R   N   NA

8. Encourages responsibility. A   S   R   N   NA

9. Encourages independence. A   S   R   N   NA

10. Understands and
    acknowledges individual
    learning styles.   A   S   R   N   NA

11. Listens to students without
    passing judgment on what
    is said.   A   S   R   N   NA

12. Understands the necessity
    of confidentiality in
    student conversations.   A   S   R   N   NA

ADDITIONAL COMMENTS

_____
_____
_____
_____
_____
_____
_____
_____
_____
_____
_____
_____
_____
_____
_____
_____
_____
_____
_____
_____
_____
_____
_____

ASSISTANT TEACHER'S SIGNATURE   TEACHER'S SIGNATURE

_____   _____

DATE   DATE

_____   _____

Your Third Stop:
Specific
Self-Evaluation

The Twelve Mighty Musts from chapter 2 appear once more. Please complete the following self-evaluation form. If you would like to share the results with your teacher, please do so. However, you may want to reflect privately.

You decide!

- Remember -

**You are striving for an "Always" response
for each
Mighty Must!**

THE PARAEDUCATOR

THE TWELVE MIGHTY MUSTS

SELF-EVALUATION

ASSISTANT TEACHER _____

TEACHER _____

DATE _____

Directions: For each item, circle the rating that **BEST** describes you. Space is provided for additional comments.

**Always   Sometimes   Rarely   Never
Not Applicable**

1. I enjoy working with others - children/adults.   A   S   R   N   NA

2. I am reliable and dependable.   A   S   R   N   NA

3. I adhere to school district sick and personal leave policies.   A   S   R   N   NA

4. I comply with the district's dress and conduct codes.   A   S   R   N   NA

5. I am flexible and adaptable.   A   S   R   N   NA

6. I exhibit self-control.   A   S   R   N   NA

7. I willingly accept constructive criticism.   A   S   R   N   NA

8. I am willing to grow professionally.   A   S   R   N   NA

9. I speak clearly.   A   S   R   N   NA

10. I write legibly.   A   S   R   N   NA

11. I spell commonly used
    words correctly.   A   S   R   N   NA

12. I work basic math
    problems correctly.   A   S   R   N   NA

I HAVE A SENSE OF HUMOR!

ALWAYS!   ALWAYS!

ALWAYS!

ADDITIONAL COMMENTS

_____
_____
_____
_____
_____
_____
_____
_____
_____
_____
_____

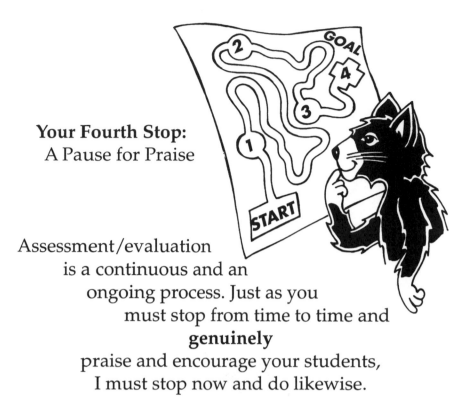

Your Fourth Stop:
A Pause for Praise

Assessment/evaluation
is a continuous and an
ongoing process. Just as you
must stop from time to time and
genuinely
praise and encourage your students,
I must stop now and do likewise.

Thank you!

Thank you!

Thank you!

You
are
the main support system
for
your
elementary classroom teacher!

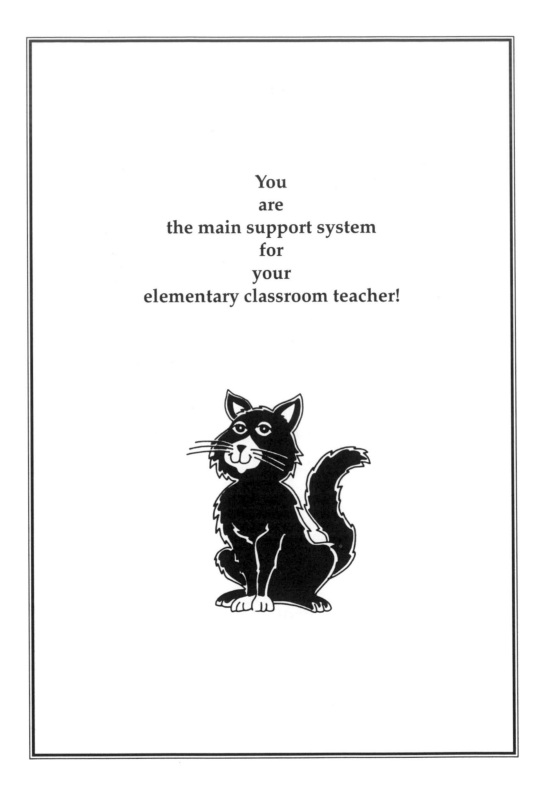

Conclusion

A conclusion need not be an end, but rather a
resting place
where one anxiously waits for
the next great adventure.

"There are no secrets to success. It is the result
of preparation, hard work, learning from failure."

- General Colin L. Powell

Did General Powell say "failure"?

Yes, he did.

The following message was published in the
Wall Street Journal by United Technologies
Corporation, Hartford, Connecticut.

Do Not Be Afraid to Fail!

You've failed many times, although you may not remember. You fell down the first time you tried to walk. You almost drowned the first time you tried to swim. Didn't you? Did you hit the ball the first time you swung a bat? Heavy hitters, the ones who hit the most home runs, also strike out a lot. R. H. Macy failed seven times before his store in New York caught on. English novelist John Creasey got 753 rejection slips before he published 564 books. Babe Ruth struck out 1,330 times, but he also hit 714 home runs. Don't worry about failure. Worry about the chances you miss when you don't even try.

I encourage you to accept your "failures"

as

challenges!

Because **you** were in the classroom today:

- **One child smiled!**
- **One child shared for the first time!**
- **One child made the lifelong connection between the spoken and the written word!**

You made positive differences in the lives of children!

_____

What you do, or what you do not do, directly affects the whole classroom environment!

As the main support system

for

the elementary classroom teacher,

what will your next

great

paraeducator

adventure

be?

_____

The decision

is

yours!

SECTION
THREE

STUDY GUIDE

SECTION THREE
STUDY GUIDE

CHAPTER 11:

1. Many elementary classroom teachers are not trained to supervise other adults in the classroom. Why?

2. Describe good supervision as defined by Houk and McKenzie.

3. List the eleven components of quality supervision according to Houk and McKenzie.

CHAPTER 12:

1. What is possibly the best tool used to measure professional growth?

2. Why is communication between the elementary classroom assistant teacher and the elementary classroom teacher vital before and after a formal evaluation?

3. Briefly explain the importance of the **Twelve Mighty Musts.**

4. Assessment/evaluation is a continuous and an ongoing process. Explain what is meant by this.

References
and
Recommended Reading

Anderson, N. A. (1989). Increasing the effectiveness of the reading aide: A guide for teachers. *Reading Horizons, 29* (3), 153-160.

Barnes, D., and Quimby, M. (1986). Analysis of prime time aide duties in selected elementary schools. *Indiana Reading Quarterly, 19* (1), 8-15.

Batzle, J. (1992). *Portfolio assessment and evaluation.* Cypress, CA: Creative Teaching Press, Inc., 10.

Billups, L. H., and Rauth, M. (1984). The new research: How effective teachers teach - Effective classroom management means more time for learning. *American Educator, 8* (2), 34-39.

Bredekamp, S. (1992) Expanded/eighth printing. *Developmentally appropriate practice in early childhood programs serving children from birth through age 8.* Washington, DC: National Association for the Education of Young Children.

Bredekamp, S., and Rosegrant, T. (1992). *Reaching potentials: Appropriate curriculum and assessment for young children.* Washington, DC: National Association for the Education of Young Children.

Brophy, J. (1985). Teacher's expectations, motives and goals for working with problem students. In Ames, C., and Ames, R., *Research on motivation in education: The classroom milieu,* 2, 175-214, Orlando, FL: Academic Press, Inc.

Carbo, M., Dunn, R., and Dunn, K. (1986). *Teaching students to read through their individual learning styles,* Englewood Cliffs, NJ: Prentice Hall, 2-3.

Carson, J. C., and Carson, P. (1984). *Any teacher can! Practical strategies for effective classroom management.* Springfield, IL: Charles C. Thomas, 132, 150-151.

Charles, C. M. (1992). *Building classroom discipline,* fourth edition. White Plains, NY: Longman Publishing Co.

Cobb, H. (1984). Assessing the role of paraprofessionals. *Spectrum, 2* (1), 37-40.

Crosser, S. (1992). Managing the early childhood classroom. *Young Children, 47* (2), 23-29.

Dishon, D., and O'Leary, P. (1994). *A guidebook for cooperative learning: A technique for creating more effective schools*, second edition. Holmes Beach, FL: Learning Publications.

Dolch, E. W. (1942). *The basic sight word test on the basic sight vocabulary*. Champaign, IL: Garrard Publishing Co.

Doyle, W. (1990). Classroom management techniques. *Student discipline strategies* (edited by Moles, O.C.). Albany, NY: State University of New York Press.

Eisele, B. (1991). *Managing the whole language classroom*. Cypress, CA: Creative Teaching Press, Inc., 62.

Elkind, D. (1989). Developmentally appropriate practice: Philosophical and practical implications. *Phi Delta Kappan, 71* (2), 113-117.

Emmer, E. T., and Hickman, J. (1991). Teacher efficacy in classroom management and discipline. *Educational and Psychological Measurement, 51* (3), 755-765.

Evertson, C. M., and Emmer, E. T. (1982). Effective management at the beginning of the school year in junior high classes. *Journal of Educational Psychology, 74* (4), 485-498.

Gettinger, M. (1988). Methods of proactive classroom management. *School Psychology Review, 17* (2), 227-242.

Gittman, B. (1989). *Safety orientation and training for teacher aides in special education classes.* Evaluation report. Westbury, NY: Nassau County Board of Cooperative Educational Services (ERIC Document Reproduction Service #ED 316 991).

Goodman, K. (1986). *What's whole in whole language?* Portsmouth, NH: Heinemann Educational Books, Inc., 34.

Grubaugh, S., and Houston, R. (1990). Establishing a classroom environment that promotes interaction and improved student behavior. *The Clearing House, 63* (8), 375-378.

Hill, S., and Hill, T. (1990). *The collaborative classroom.* Portsmouth, NH: Heinemann Educational Books, Inc., 1-6.

Houk, C. S., and McKenzie, R. (1986). Use of paraprofessionals in the resource room. *Exceptional
Children, 53* (1), 41-45.

Houk, C. S., and McKenzie, R. (1988).
Paraprofessionals - Training for the classroom.
Circle Pines, MN: American Guidance
Service.

Jarolimek, J., and Parker, W. C. (1993). *Social studies
in elementary education.* New York, NY:
Macmillan Publishing Co.

Keefe, S. D. (1981). Is your aide your partner?
Academic Therapy, 17 (1), 89-90.

Lacattiva, C. (1985, March 22-26). *The use of parapro-
fessionals as part of the teaching team.* Paper pre-
sented at the annual meeting of the
Association for Supervision and Curriculum
Development, Chicago, IL (ERIC Document
Reproduction Service #ED 258 325).

Lasley, T. J. (1989). A teacher development model
for classroom management. *Phi Delta Kappan,
71* (1), 36-38.

Moles, O. C. (1990). *Student discipline strategies,
research and practice.* Albany, NY: State
University of New York Press.

National Council of Teachers of Mathematics, Curriculum and Evaluation Standards for School Mathematics (1989). Reston, VA: NCTM, Inc., 5-6.

Page, D. R. (1994). *A study of the differences in efficacy ratings of elementary classroom assistant teachers who did and did not receive training in classroom management strategies* (Doctoral dissertation, University of Mississippi). ProQuest - Dissertation Abstracts, order # AAC 9431577.

Pickett, A. L., Vasa, S. F., and Steckelberg, A. L. (1993). *Using paraeducators effectively in the classroom*. Bloomington, IN: Phi Delta Kappa Educational Foundation, Fastback # 358, 7.

Schwartz, S., and Pollishuke, M. (1991). *Creating the child-centered classroom*. Katonah, NY: Richard C. Owen Publishers, Inc.

Strachan, P. (1990). *A training program for paraprofessionals: Classroom management skills*. Practicum, Nova University (ERIC Document Reproduction Service #ED 325 233).

Teachers Network News (1990). Cambridge, MA: Harvard Graduate School of Education.

Van De Walle, J. A. (1990). *Elementary School Mathematics: Teaching Developmentally*. White Plains, NY: Longman Publishing Co.

Victor, E. (1989). *Science for the elementary school,* sixth edition. New York, NY: Macmillan Publishing Co.

Wolfe, P. (1988). *Classroom management and catch them being good.* A staff development program. Alexandria, VA: Association for Supervision and Curriculum Development (ASCD).

Wolfgang, C. H., and Wolfgang, M. E. (1992). *School for young children, developmentally appropriate practices.* Needham Heights, MA: Allyn and Bacon.

Womack, S. T. (1987). How to maximize the use of a teacher's aide. *The Clearing House, 31* (3), 331.

Woolfolk, A. E. (1987). Specific guidelines for using praise appropriately. *Educational Psychology,* Third Edition. Englewood Cliffs, NJ: Prentice Hall.

About the Author

Diane Page began her teaching career in the late 1960s in Houston, Texas. She has taught all grades, prekindergarten through grade 5, and adult literacy courses at the community college level. She has served as an instructor in the School of Education at the University of Mississippi. Diane holds a bachelor's degree in elementary education from Mississippi State University, a master's degree and a doctor of philosophy degree in elementary education from the University of Mississippi.

Currently, Diane is president of The Teacher's Assistant Group, Inc., Educational Consultants of Tupelo, Mississippi. She also serves as adjunct professor with the University of Mississippi, Tupelo campus. She is known throughout her state as a staunch political advocate for paraeducators.

About the Illustrator

An award winning commercial artist, Bruce Bigelow owns the Sundown Studio, located in the country about six miles from downtown Tupelo, Mississippi. Bruce earned a bachelor of fine arts degree from Kansas University with a major in commercial art. In addition to graphic design, he is a portrait artist. His portraits and paintings are displayed in homes and in businesses throughout the United States.

Bruce's career has spanned forty-one years, during which he has been dedicated to graphic as well as fine art. As a graphic artist, Bruce specializes in illustration, design, copy, and supervises his work from concept to finished product.

THE

PARAEDUCATOR

NOTEBOOK

About the Paraeducator Notebook

The notebook is designed for you to use
year after year.

1. Run copies of every page.

2. Punch holes on the left side of the copies
   using a three-hole punch.

3. Insert the copies into a soft or hardback
   notebook.

Handy patterns

are found in your notebook.

Handy patterns have many uses.

They may be enlarged for your specific purpose.

Here are a few suggestions:

1. Bulletin board borders

2. Clip art for a bulletin board focus

3. Math manipulatives

4. Covers for student-written books

5. Inside sheets for student-written books

If possible, always laminate paper.

- A great time-saver -

PROFESSIONAL INFORMATION

MY NAME_____

ADDRESS_____

_____

_____

TELEPHONE NUMBER_____

EMERGENCY CONTACT PERSON_____

TELEPHONE NUMBER_____

MY TEACHER'S NAME_____

ADDRESS_____

_____

_____

TELEPHONE NUMBER_____

EMERGENCY CONTACT PERSON_____

TELEPHONE NUMBER_____

SCHOOL INFORMATION

SCHOOL NAME_____

ADDRESS_____

_____

_____

TELEPHONE NUMBERS_____

_____

_____

PRINCIPAL'S NAME_____

VICE PRINCIPAL'S NAME_____

SECRETARY'S NAME_____

OTHER IMPORTANT INFORMATION

_____

_____

_____

_____

_____

_____

_____

_____

_____

_____

SCHOOL INFORMATION

Student's Name	Address	Home Phone No.	Parents' Names	Emergency Phone No.

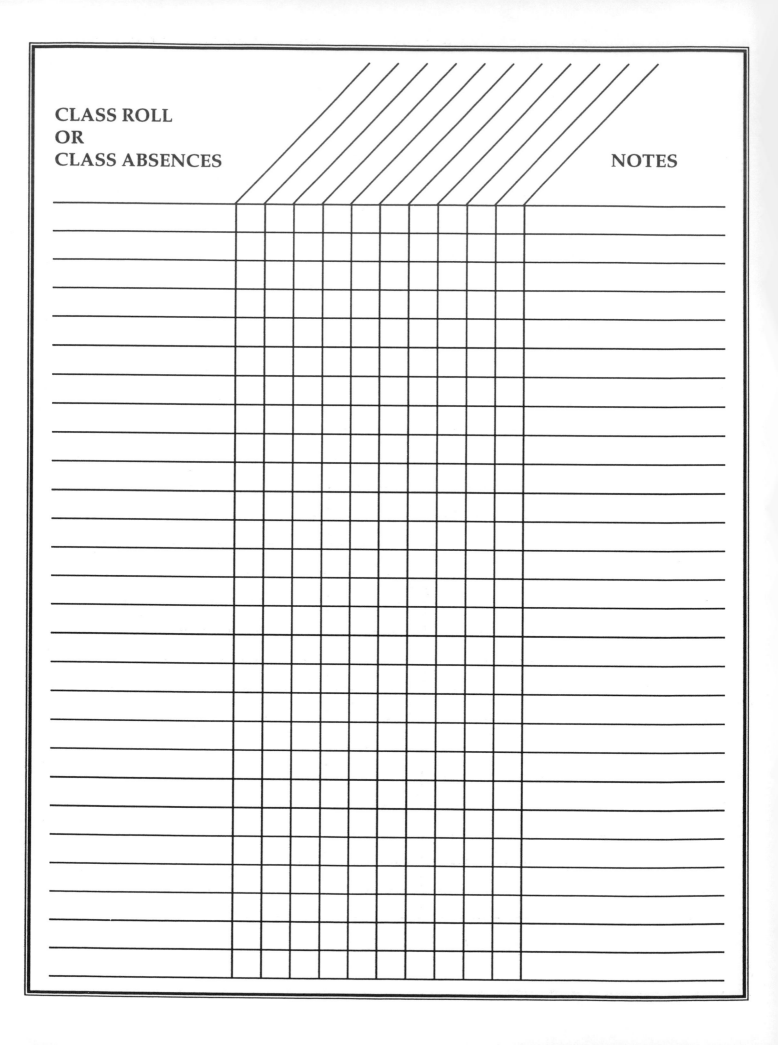

CLASS ROLL
OR
CLASS ABSENCES

NOTES

SUBJECT _____

CLASS _____

1.																				
2.																				
3.																				
4.																				
5.																				
6.																				
7.																				
8.																				
9.																				
10.																				
11.																				
12.																				
13.																				
14.																				
15.																				
16.																				
17.																				
18.																				
19.																				
20.																				
21.																				
22.																				
23.																				
24.																				
25.																				
26.																				

LESSON PLAN

SUBJECT_____

DATE_____

NUMBER OF STUDENTS_____

· ·

OBJECTIVE_____

_____

_____

_____

_____

_____

_____

_____

PROCEDURE_____

_____

_____

_____

_____

_____

_____

_____

_____

_____

_____

_____

MATERIALS_____

_____

_____

_____

_____

_____

_____

_____

EVALUATION_____

_____

_____

_____

_____

_____

_____

REMARKS

OBSERVATION FORM
"KID WATCHING"

NAME OF STUDENT_____

DATE_____

TIME_____

PURPOSE_____

ACTIVITY_____

OBSERVATION

_____

_____

_____

_____

_____

_____

_____

_____

_____

_____

_____

_____

REMARKS

THE

CAPABLE

COMPETENT

PARAEDUCATOR

MONTHLY

PLANNER

AUGUST

SUNDAY	MONDAY	TUESDAY	WEDNESDAY	THURSDAY	FRIDAY	SATURDAY

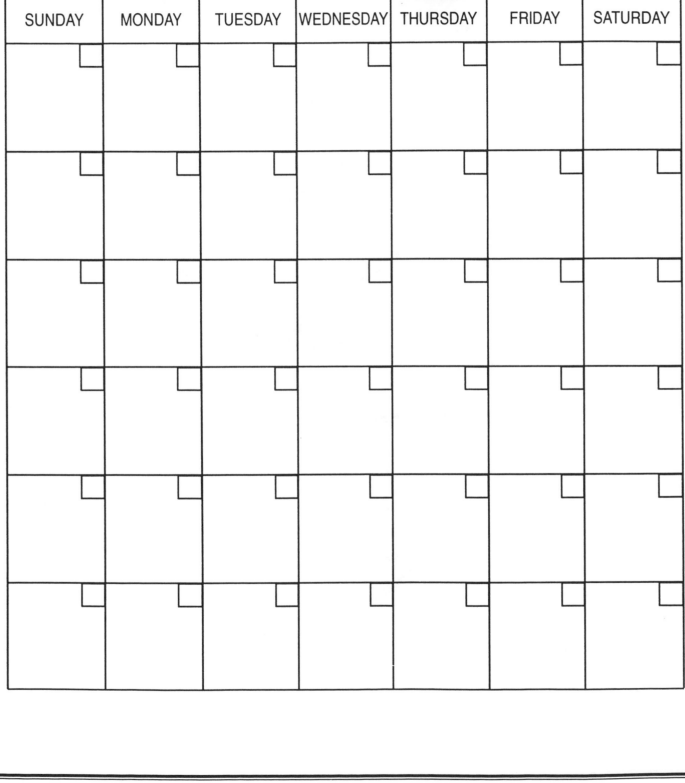

SEPTEMBER

SUNDAY	MONDAY	TUESDAY	WEDNESDAY	THURSDAY	FRIDAY	SATURDAY

COUNT TO 100

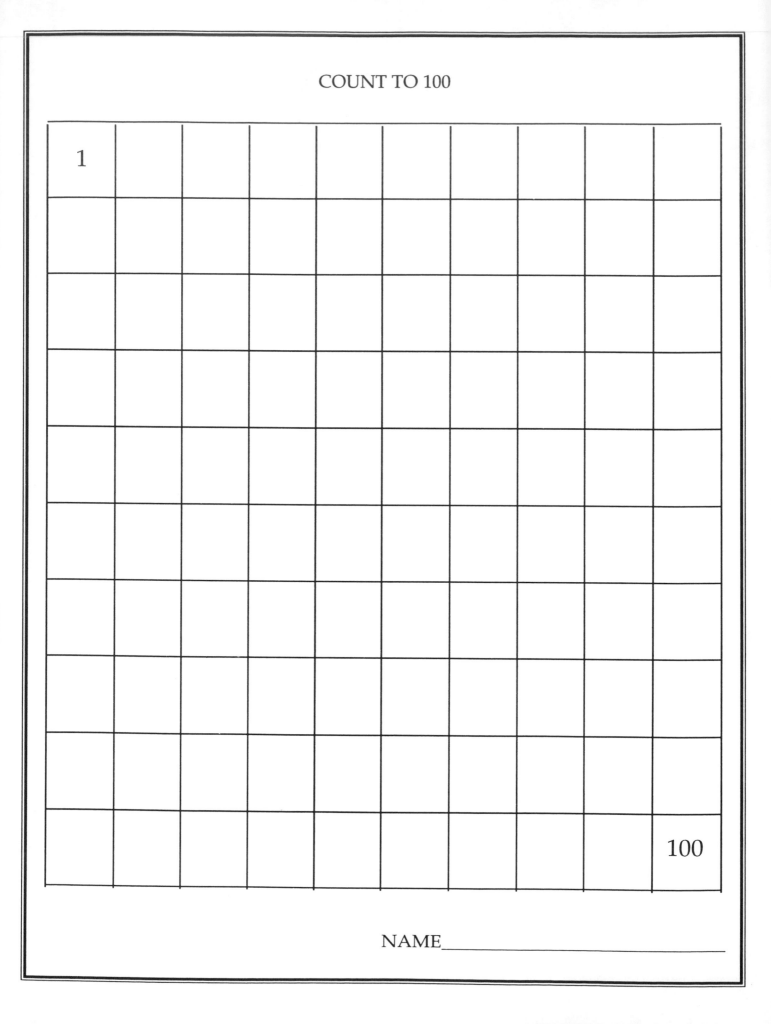

1									
									100

NAME_____

ADDITION GRID

	0	1	2	3	4	5	6	7	8	9	10
0											
1				4							
2											
3											13
4											
5											
6							12				
7											
8										17	
9											
10				13							

NAME_____

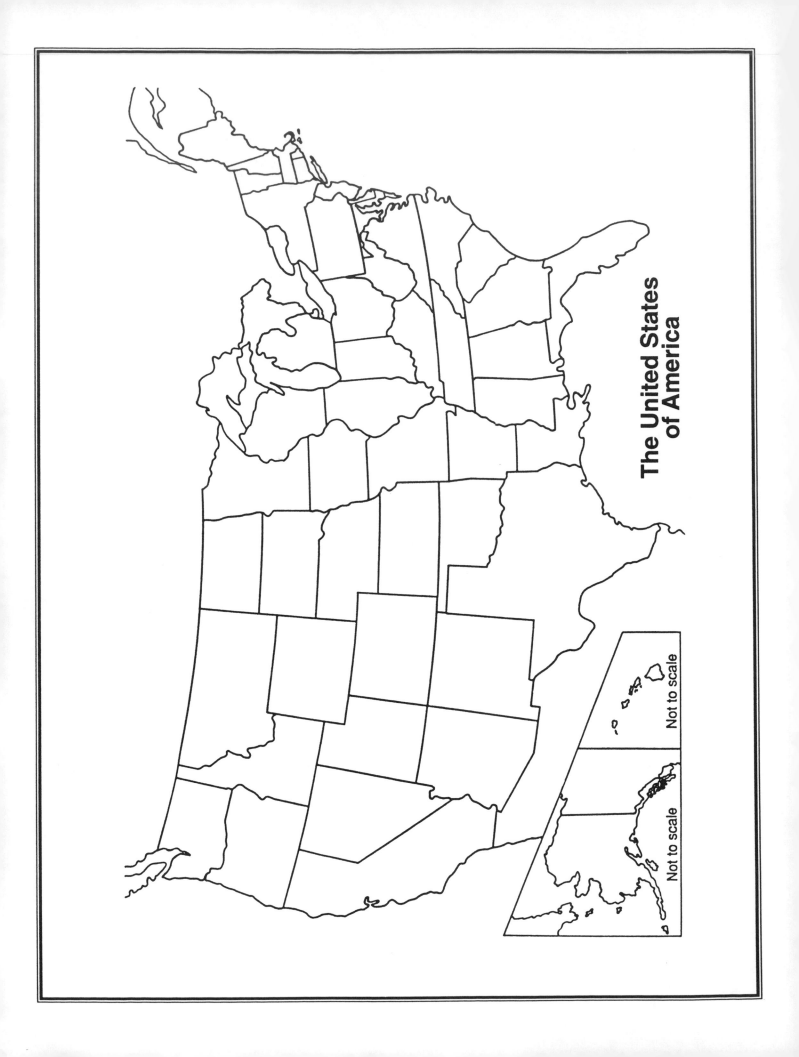

The United States
of America

Not to scale

Not to scale

OCTOBER

SUNDAY	MONDAY	TUESDAY	WEDNESDAY	THURSDAY	FRIDAY	SATURDAY

pumpkins

NOVEMBER

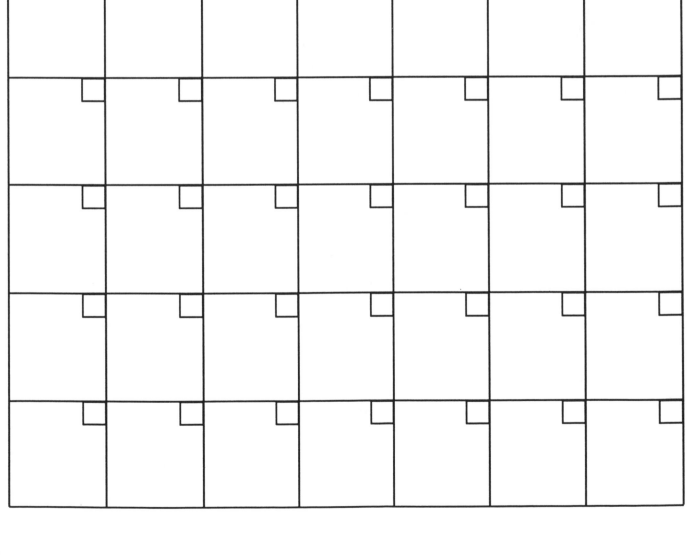

SUNDAY	MONDAY	TUESDAY	WEDNESDAY	THURSDAY	FRIDAY	SATURDAY

DECEMBER

SUNDAY	MONDAY	TUESDAY	WEDNESDAY	THURSDAY	FRIDAY	SATURDAY

MERRY CHRISTMAS

HAPPY HANUKKAH

Dear Santa,

_____
_____
_____
_____
_____
_____
_____
_____
_____
_____
_____
_____
_____
_____
_____
_____
_____
_____
_____

from,

_____

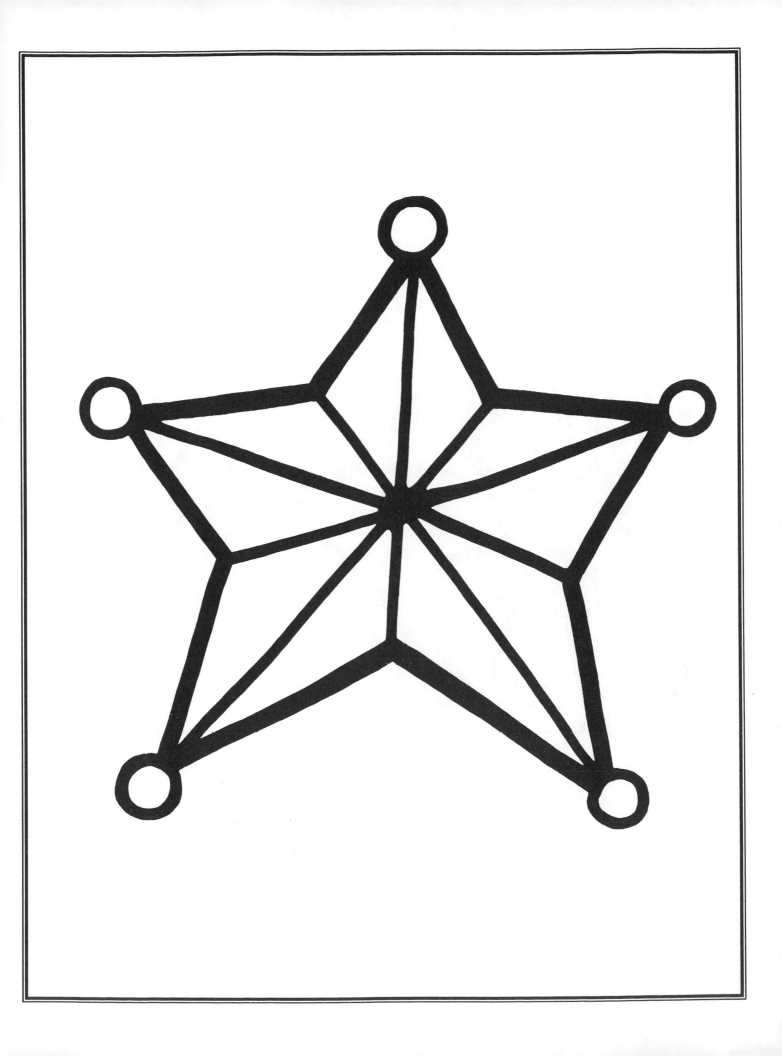

My Christmas Shopping List

JANUARY

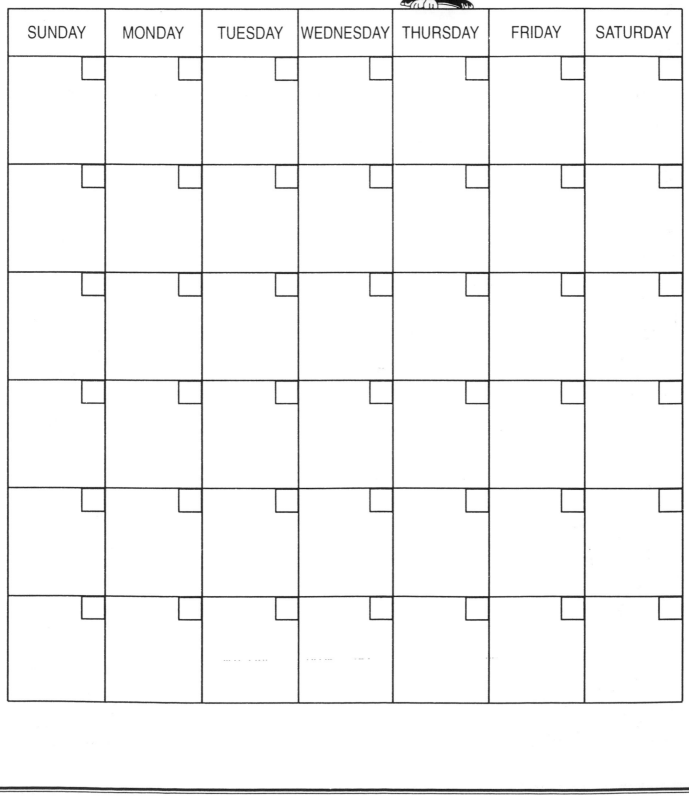

SUNDAY	MONDAY	TUESDAY	WEDNESDAY	THURSDAY	FRIDAY	SATURDAY

New Year's Resolutions

FEBRUARY

SUNDAY	MONDAY	TUESDAY	WEDNESDAY	THURSDAY	FRIDAY	SATURDAY

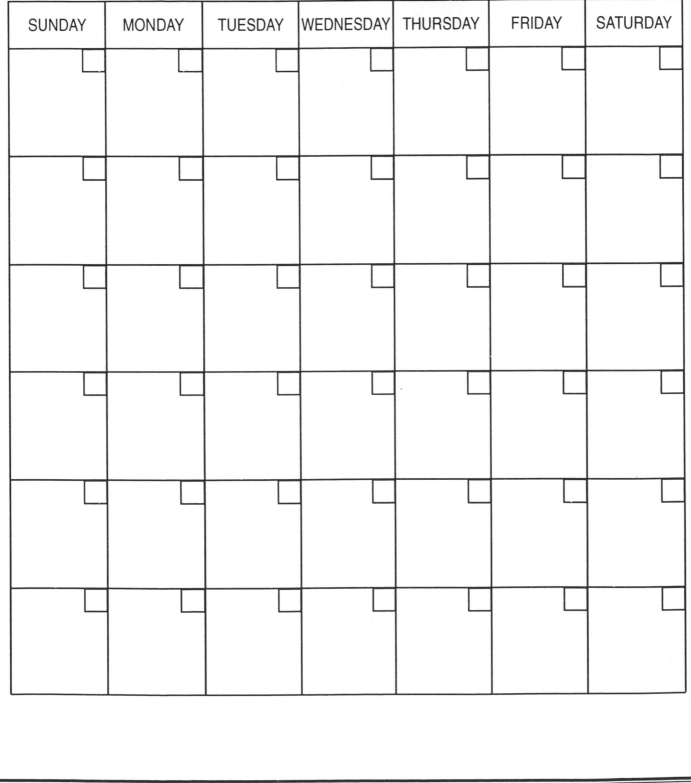

MARCH

SUNDAY	MONDAY	TUESDAY	WEDNESDAY	THURSDAY	FRIDAY	SATURDAY

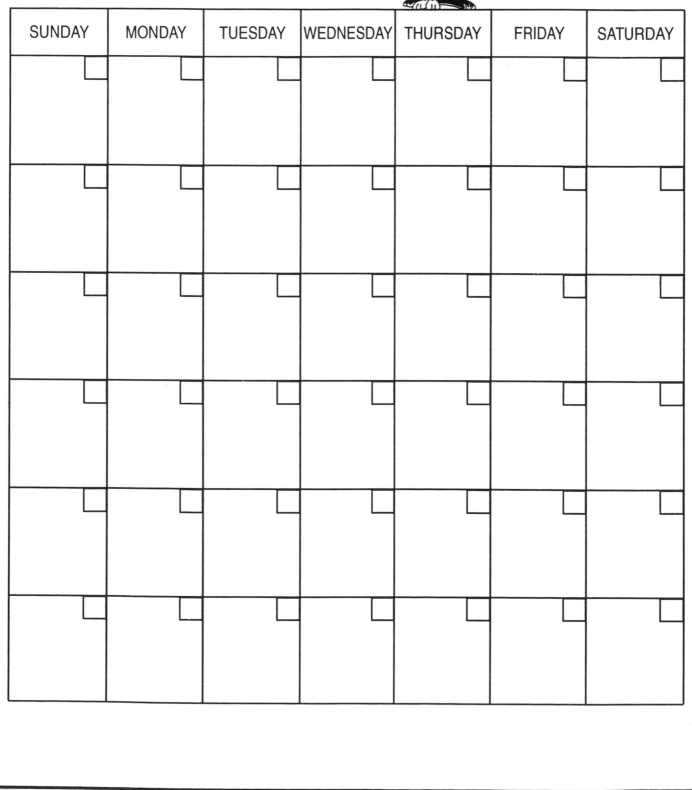

MATH

GRAPH THE ACTION!

NAME THAT GRAPH ——————————————————————————————

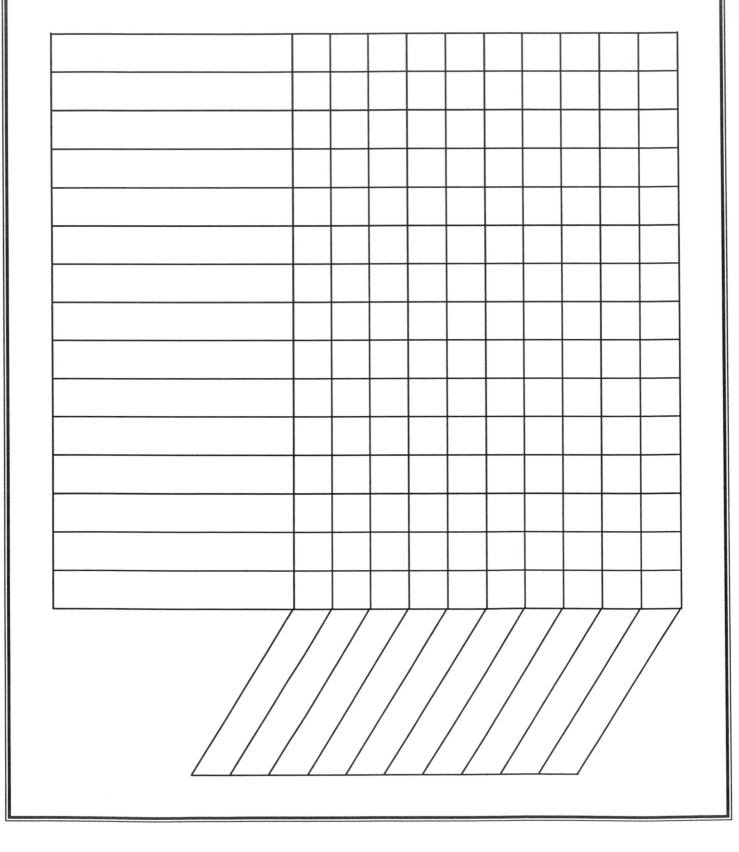

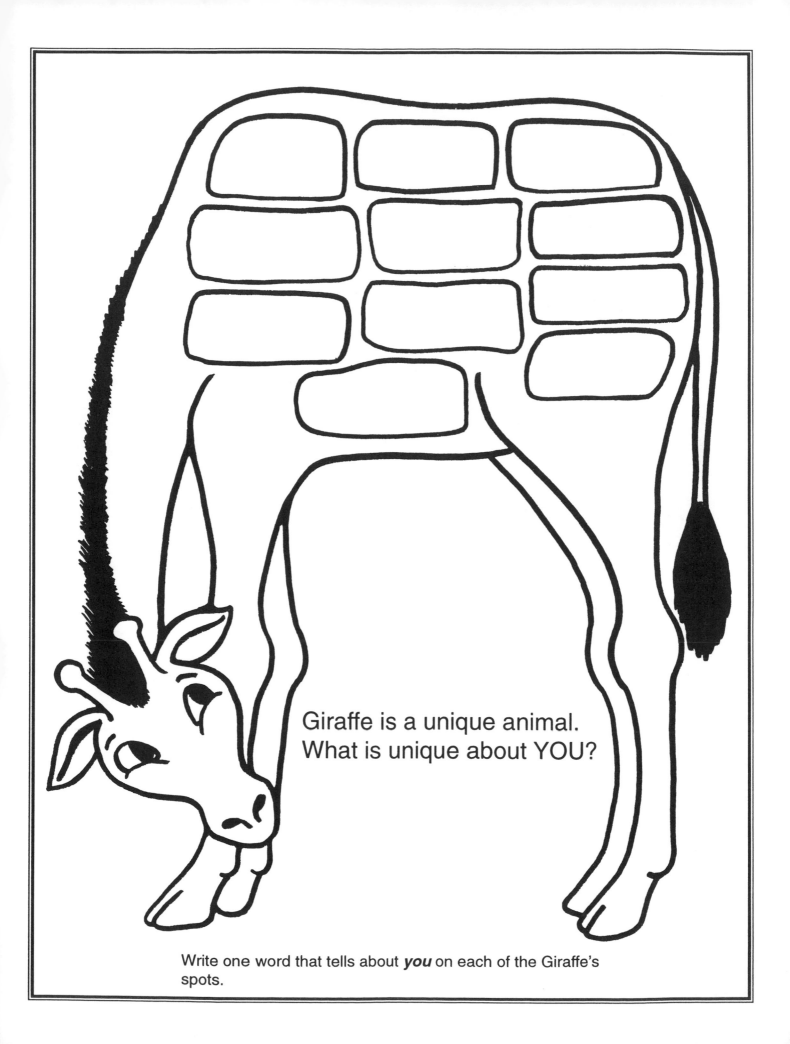

Giraffe is a unique animal.
What is unique about YOU?

Write one word that tells about **you** on each of the Giraffe's spots.

APRIL

SUNDAY	MONDAY	TUESDAY	WEDNESDAY	THURSDAY	FRIDAY	SATURDAY

APRIL'S

POETRY

MAY

SUNDAY	MONDAY	TUESDAY	WEDNESDAY	THURSDAY	FRIDAY	SATURDAY

Fold on dotted lines.

MULTIPLICATION GRID

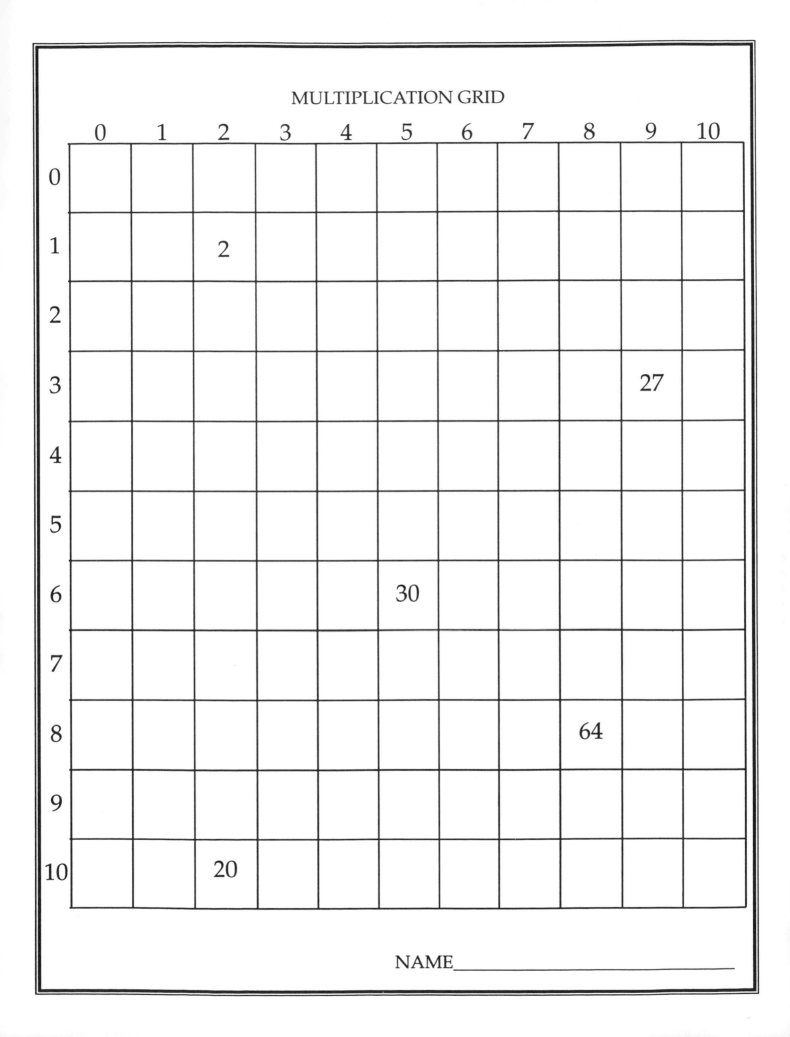

	0	1	2	3	4	5	6	7	8	9	10
0											
1			2								
2											
3										27	
4											
5											
6						30					
7											
8									64		
9											
10			20								

NAME_____

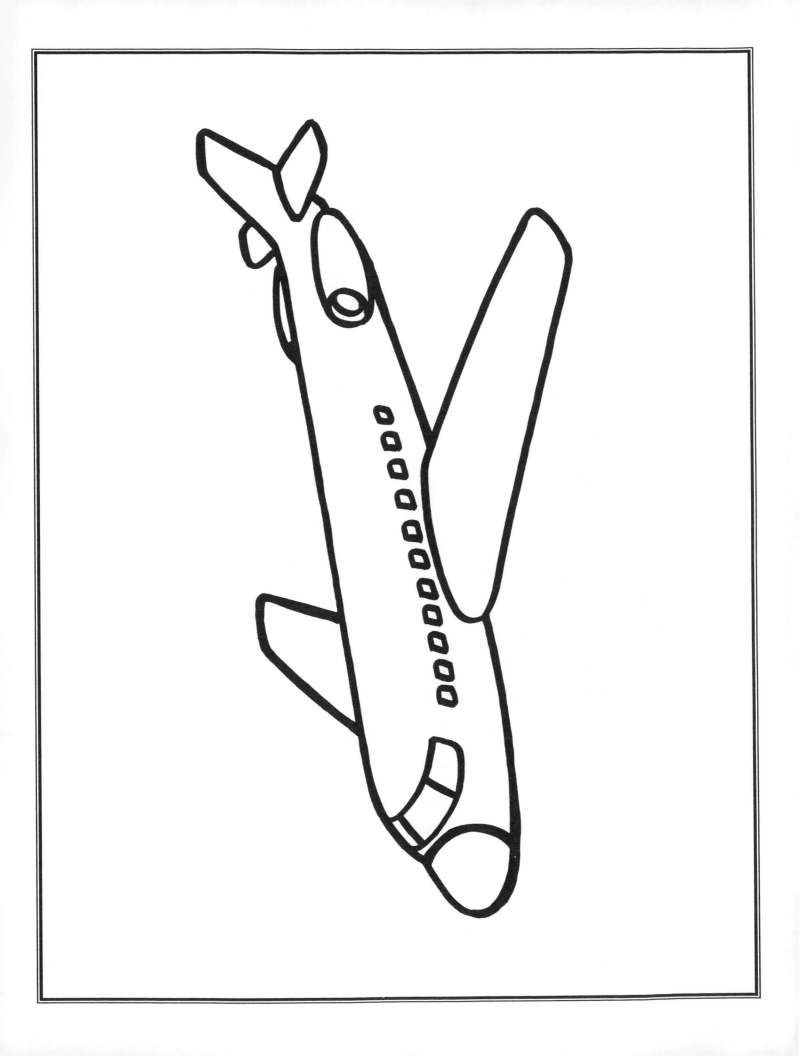

JUNE

SUNDAY	MONDAY	TUESDAY	WEDNESDAY	THURSDAY	FRIDAY	SATURDAY

Message To Parents

Happy Birthday to You!!!

to _____

from _____

Happy Birthday!

to

from

ANNOUNCING

Event _____

Date _____

Time _____

Place _____

Message _____

_____

Fold on dotted lines.

SUCCESS-O-GRAM

_____

_____

_____

_____

_____

_____

_____

CERTIFICATE OF ACHIEVEMENT

Strike Up The Band for

_____

who is doing excellent work in

_____

signature   date

_____

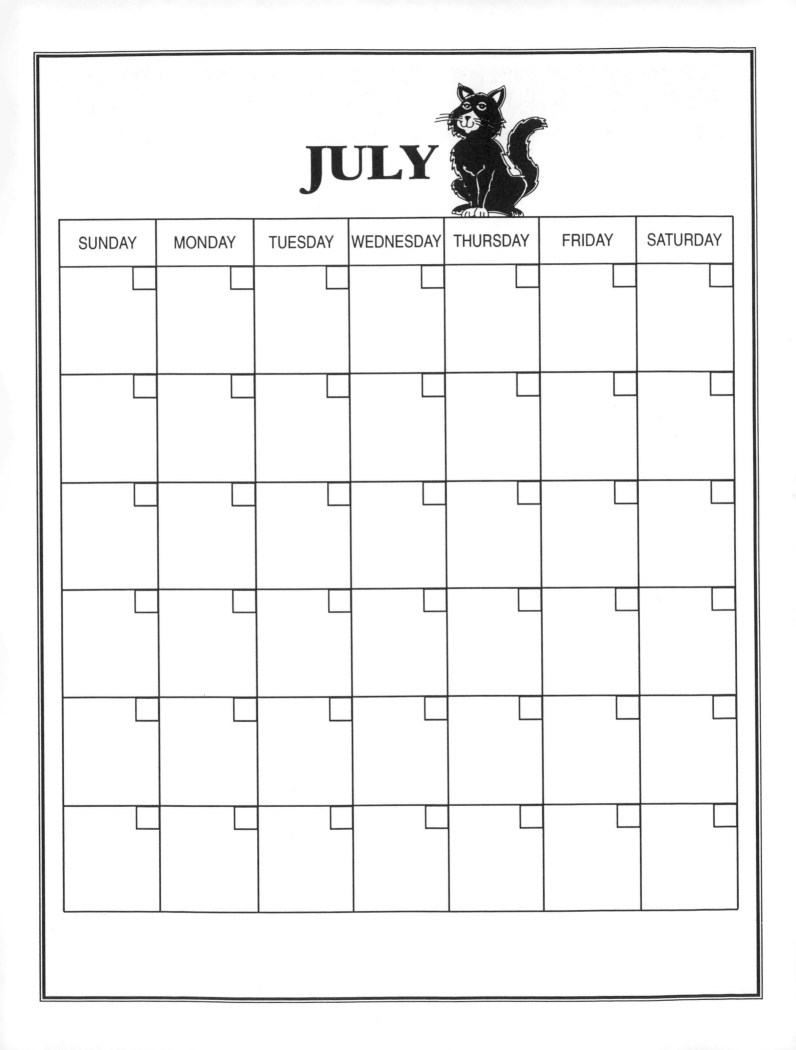

JULY

SUNDAY	MONDAY	TUESDAY	WEDNESDAY	THURSDAY	FRIDAY	SATURDAY

HOT OFF THE PRESS

MY TO DO LIST

- [ ] _____
- [ ] _____
- [ ] _____
- [ ] _____
- [ ] _____
- [ ] _____
- [ ] _____
- [ ] _____
- [ ] _____
- [ ] _____

ALL PURPOSE CHART

A Reminder to Parents

Dear _____

Don't forget! This is important! _____

_____

_____

_____

_____

_____

_____

_____
Signature   Date

_____
Phone #

A Note of Thanks...
In Appreciation for What You Have Done!

_____

_____

_____

_____

_____

_____

_____
Signature

_____
Date